T0271119

AMERICAN FOREIGN AFFAIRS

A Compact History

GORDON TULLOCK

George Mason University, USA

AMERICAN FOREIGN AFFAIRS

A Compact History

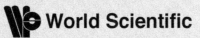 **World Scientific**

NEW JERSEY · LONDON · SINGAPORE · BEIJING · SHANGHAI · HONG KONG · TAIPEI · CHENNAI

Published by

World Scientific Publishing Co. Pte. Ltd.

5 Toh Tuck Link, Singapore 596224

USA office: 27 Warren Street, Suite 401-402, Hackensack, NJ 07601

UK office: 57 Shelton Street, Covent Garden, London WC2H 9HE

Library of Congress Cataloging-in-Publication Data
Tullock, Gordon.
  American foreign affairs : a compact history / by Gordon Tullock.
    p. cm.
  Includes bibliographical references and index.
  ISBN-13: 978-981-283-507-9 (softcover : alk. paper)
  ISBN-10: 981-283-507-5 (softcover : alk. paper)
  1. United States--Foreign relations. I. Title.

E183.7.T85 2009
327.73--dc22

                                                    2008049858

British Library Cataloguing-in-Publication Data
A catalogue record for this book is available from the British Library.

Typeset by Stallion Press
Email: enqueries@stallionpress.com

Printed in Singapore.

Preface

As a background to this book, let me begin with some brief auto-biographical notes to explain why I feel qualified to write on foreign affairs although most of my work has been devoted to the internal functioning of the state. All my life I have been more interested in foreign affairs than in almost anything else. In high school, I followed the foreign news intensively and, even though I was studying law, did so also in the University. In a way I played an active role in foreign affairs since I was drafted into the army and trained as an infantry rifleman. Although I landed in Normandy on D plus seven, and crossed the Remagen bridge on the first night, my luck held out, and I was never within rifle range of any German soldier.

On return to the United States, I returned to the law school and on graduation, I took a job in a small law firm in downtown Chicago. Pursuing my hobby, however, I had passed the Foreign Service exam, and after four months of legal practice, I joined the Foreign Service. I now think that my interest in foreign affairs in a way disqualified me for success in that profession. The people who got ahead rapidly in the Foreign Service were those who concentrated their studies on the higher levels of the Department of State rather than a given foreign country. In any case it shows in my career. I selected China as my field of activity for my first assignment. This was another mistake since I am, as I did not then know, partially tone deaf and hence could never really learn Chinese. My efforts to learn Chinese at places like Yale and Cornell were unavailing.

While I was studying law in Chicago, I took the required one quarter course[1] under Henry Simons in economics. Although I did not anticipate it at the time, this changed my whole life. I began as a hobby pursuing economics as well as foreign affairs. While studying Chinese at Yale, I entered the Coop one day and picked up a book entitled "Human Action" by Von Mises. Although I remained a good Chicagoan in my views, this book and my later personal acquaintance with its author pushed me even farther into economics.

The early part of "Human Action" is devoted to methodology and in Von Mises' view similar methods could be applied in other fields. At the time I was employed in a large and inefficient bureaucracy, the Department of State. Further, I had had an opportunity to observe two other inefficient bureaucracies, the Nationalist and the Communist governments of China. I also had done some reading in history and was aware of the fact that China under the Empire had had a generally successful bureaucracy.

I decided to write a book on bureaucracy which would be radically different from the existing and in my opinion, inferior books then in

---

[1] The draft board shortened my studies on economics by one week.

existence. I started while still in the Foreign Service although fully occupied in writing other things for the Department such as analyses of politics in Korea.

I was not doing very well in the Foreign Service. Although I was always a member of the aristocracy as a political officer, I imagine I would eventually have been either selected out or sent to minor posts in Africa. As a matter of fact, I resigned and went off to California to write my book. I had, rather by accident, at this time formed a connection with Karl Popper and I intended to use him as an asset in writing the book. This turned out to the impossible, because Karl was deeply involved in translating his basic methodological book. Nevertheless, I learned a great deal from my contact with him and my first book, "Inside Bureaucracy" was markedly improved by his influence. It needed improvement. For many years I couldn't get it published, and when I finally broke through that barrier it sold badly.[2]

I can, nevertheless, claim considerable influence in the development of the modern theory of bureaucracy since both Anthony Downs and William Niskanen read the manuscript and drew on it heavily in their own books. I believe the basic reason that they sold well and my book did not is simply that they were much less radical than I.

After I resigned from the Foreign Service, I had about a year in which I held minor jobs and worked on my book. Eventually, I was offered

---

[2] It has recently been reprinted.

a job in a newly created Department of International Studies at the University of South Carolina. The job was offered to me by Richard Walker who was one of the very rare members of the then China studies profession who, like me, detested the Chinese Communists. He had, in fact, been fired from Yale because of his differences from the rest of the faculty on this point.

I had, however, had copies of the manuscript *Inside Bureaucracy* duplicated and circulated them. One of them went to the University of Virginia and they offered me a postdoctoral fellowship for one year. Walker generously permitted me to leave for that year and then return to South Carolina.

I learned a good deal more economics at the University of Virginia and began publishing in economic journals. My first important article essentially involved both economics and political science, and introduced the scientific examination of log rolling to economics and political science.

On completion of my one year there, I returned to the University of South Carolina and to the teaching of international studies. I had, however, while in Virginia, produced an eighty-page monograph on political applications to economics which eventually became the core of the Calculus of Consent.

Nevertheless, I continued to be highly interested in foreign affairs, even though my academic publishing from then on, concerned economic and political matters as well as strictly international studies topics.

In this book then, I return to my first love and attempt to convert what is otherwise a hobby into a serious study. Whither I succeed or not, the readers will have to judge for themselves. I can honestly say that I'm satisfied, but like most authors, I'm aware of the difference between my preference function and that of the readers, to say nothing of that of the reviewers. I, therefore, leave the book in the hands of its critics. I hope, but do not expect, they will view it kindly.

Contents

Chapter 1

Purposes of Foreign Policy

I should like to start by recounting a very unusual research project which I undertook, and which turned out to raise more questions than answers. I began asking people what they thought the objective of the United States' foreign policy should be. Most of them were U.S. citizens, and the question I asked was a very simple request for their view of the desirable objective for the U.S. policy. In a few cases, I asked the question of foreigners and in those cases, I asked the objective which they felt would be suitable for their country.

In most cases, it was obvious that the respondents had not thought much about the subject. This is surprisingly granted that the newspapers, television, and almost all other channels of public communication devote a great deal of attention to foreign affairs. It is normal for the people who produce these communications either to approve of or disapprove of the policies they discuss. Normally, however, this is expressed simply as approval or disapproval and not as a statement that the new policy will or will not advance some major objective. Presumably, there is an objective in the back of the person's mind, but perhaps, he thinks it is so obvious that it does not need to be put in words.

Nevertheless, my experiment, generally speaking, turned up nothing. There were a few exceptions; a few people said the objective should be Peace. Since I asked this question and got these answers during the Iraqi unpleasantness, this was somewhat surprising. Further of the particular people who said this should be the objective, none wanted withdrawal from Iraq. (This was during the early part of the U.S. operations). They might have thought that the long run effect of the Iraqi war would be peace, although it's not obvious why they thought so. Further at the time that I was asking the question, the nastiness in Darfur was not only continuing, but getting a good deal of attention in the media. As far as I could see, insofar as the people I asked had any ideas at all about this, they thought that somebody should send in troops and stop it. This cast doubt on whether my respondents were all that peaceful.

Another answer which I got from one person, and that person, an economics professor, was that the objective should be to increase American per capita income. I think most people would buy that for governmental policy in general, but didn't think of that particular objective in connection with foreign policy. If I asked what the objective of the domestic policy was, I might have received many endorsements of that same objective.

The problem of increasing per capita income is the decision as to who should be included in the "capita". At the moment, the United States is receiving very large numbers of Mexican immigrants. They pretty invariably increase their living standard when they arrive, but that doesn't mean that the per capita income of the country goes up. In fact the arrival of a large number of inexpensive laborers lowers it. A great many of them take jobs in unskilled activities like waiters. Since I normally eat out, this has improved my living standard since the service is better and cheaper. It obviously improves their living standard, but what about the living standard of other Americans who want a job as a waiter in a restaurant?

Assuming that the Mexicans are efficient, there are three effects on living standards, the living standard of the Mexicans who remain in Mexico rises because the labor capital ratio shifts in favor of labor. The immigrants presumably gain or they would not immigrate. The wages of those Americans who are displaced by them, or who continue working as a waiter, but at a lower wage, fall.

Whether this change increases per capita income of the United States depends on who are included in the capita. Certainly, it increases the total income of the United States and the total income of the Mexicans, because many of them are now in the United States. The world per capita income goes up, even if many Americans have their income lowered. This reduction in U. S. wages is presumably the reason that labor unions in 1923 pushed so hard for immigration restrictions. It seems likely that the weakening of the effective restrictions on immigration reflects to a considerable extent a general weakening of the organized labor movement in the United States. They are no longer able to insist on American wages being higher than an immigrant would accept.

As a reader will see in subsequent chapters of my book, another part of American policy did, indeed, improve the living standard of the Americans. They pursued an unremitting policy of aggressive wars against the Indians up to about 1890. The subject will be discussed in more detail below, but it provided *Lebensraum* for the Americans and hence they were more prosperous. Before 1923, they welcomed large numbers of immigrants with the important exception of Chinese, and Japanese who were restricted. In 1923, political pressure mainly by labor unions led to the establishment of a quota system for immigration.

This quota system was formally justified on the grounds that the bulk of their older citizen groups came from north-western Europe. The new emigrants were very largely from south-eastern Europe. In fact many of them were Jews, although, if my recollection is correct, this was not mentioned in the justification of the quotas. When I was in high school, the civics course contained a short section on this, entirely in terms of preserving the traditional culture rather than having it diluted by people from Russia,

Poland, and (to a lesser extent) Italy. If my recollection is right, there was absolutely no sign of objection to this obviously racist policy among either the students or the teachers.

The quotas were so arranged that the number of permissible immigrants from places like England was much higher than the number of people who actually wanted to come. On the other hand, places like Poland had a great excess of people who wanted to come to the United States. Thus, the actual number of immigrants to the United States was much lower than the total which the quotas would have admitted had they not had these national sub quotas.

As I said the labor unions had pushed the system through politically, and their members were major gainers from it. It was during this period that American living standards became so much higher than those in Europe and, no doubt, the quota system was important in that. The large scale immigration of Mexicans has lowered the difference between their living standard and that of western Europe.

In the 1960s, however, there was a further change. A bill was passed permitting people legally residing in the United States to bring in their relatives as legal immigrants. The sponsor of the bill said that it would bring in perhaps 60,000 persons. It set up, however, a chain system. The new immigrants brought in by this system could then bring in their relatives, thus the quota system was undermined.

At the same time, and this is rather mysterious, the enforcement of restrictions on illegal immigration fell sharply. The principal effect was the flooding of Mexicans into the United States. The enforcement was weak, but it did mean that many of these illegal immigrants found it necessary to run the risk of crossing the deserts in the south-western United States. How many died is unknown. That many made it is obvious if you look at American restaurants, or construction jobs. There are also a number of these immigrants employed in farms or factories.

From the standpoint of the existing American labor, this is undesirable and their living standards have not risen as fast as they would have without this competition. To repeat, in a way this effect, I suppose, is a secondary consequence of the weakening of the labor unions. Their members are now a much smaller share of employed Americans and of people eligible to vote. Hence, their inability to limit this competition is readily understandable.

Chapter 2

Historical Background

Before giving the history of the U.S. foreign policy, I would like to devote some pages to the situation before the United States was born as a nation. Their early history was heavily affected by things which had happened before Columbus sailed the ocean blue.

The powerful Roman Empire had fallen and the general level of civilization in Europe underwent a very sharp retrogression. That was 1000 years before Columbus and by his day, there had been very considerable recovery from the disaster. The Empire, however, had not been successfully reconstructed. Europe was divided among a number of small countries which were in almost continuous war with each other.

David Hume, observing the situation, revived the theory of balance of power first mentioned by Thucydides. He argued that the rise in power of any given state would frighten other states so that a coalition against it would be created. As an extreme example, when Charles V, heading a largely Catholic league, won his great victory at Mulheim, several of his Catholic allies promptly changed sides and joined in alliance with the Protestant kingdoms.

The balance of power is apparently not a universal phenomenon. Not only did Rome overcome it, but it was not successful in China. China is about the same size as Europe, and from time to time the ruling dynasty would collapse. This would lead to a situation in which various generals and provincial governors attempted to establish new dynasties in their own family. This led to civil wars for which the period from 1911 to 1950, will do as a recent example. This was called the period of "warlords". The war between the various contending military leaders normally ended in one winning and establishing a new dynasty rather than in the balance of power preventing that.

Why the balance of power prevented unification in Europe, but did not prevent it in China, I do not really know, but I have a theoretical suggestion. China was a hydraulic society with extensive irrigation canals which could also be used by boats. Thus, transportation between different parts of China was generally much easier than between, let's say, Paris and Madrid. This would tend to make movement of military forces much easier and hence, benefit large states. The decisive battle which established Ming was actually a naval battle fought on an inland lake with the forces reaching the lake by canals. The reader may not regard this as a very good theory, and I must confess that the author is hardly certain of it.

Let's now turn to the new world. When Columbus reached the Antilles, which he thought were islands off the coast of China, Ferdinand V, and then his successor, Charles V, were much more interested in Europe than in developing this new area. They actually passed laws restricting migration to it. Fortunately, these laws were not stringently enforced. From the perspective of the present day, this looks close to insane, but then it seemed a sensible thing to do. Ferdinand V actually thought that Spain was under populated. There were efforts to explore the island chain and to some extent the mainland, but they were minor and feeble until Hernán Cortez's conquest.

There were actually efforts to prevent development on the mainland and an expedition was sent out for the purpose of arresting Cortez and bringing him back for trial. Cortez was able to convince the soldiers in the expedition that they would be better off joining him in conquering Mexico than taking him back in chains. Those of them who survived *la noche triste* were indeed better off.

Although Cortez's success encouraged further exploration in the Western Hemisphere, the government in Spain seemed to have thought of it mainly as a source of silver to maintain their armies in Europe. Cortez himself, however, was properly rewarded. He married into a noble family in Spain, was made a Marquis, and given a massive estate in Mexico.

Francisco Pizarro did not do as well although the amount of gold and silver he sent to Spain was greater than that sent by Cortez. In his case, his expedition was not actually opposed by the Spanish government in the new world, but was also not particularly encouraged. It was essentially a free enterprise operation. After his conquest, however, he not only faced a successful mutiny among his soldiers, who killed him, but his family fell into disfavor with the King. Every male member was eliminated.

Although the Spanish government did little to encourage the development of their new American colonies, and indeed did a good deal to make it hard to develop them, nonetheless, there were many colonists and the large area, now speaking Spanish, in the Western Hemisphere developed into relatively prosperous colonies.

I have skipped over the Portuguese development, so let's turn to them now. Under the leadership of Henry, the navigator, the Portuguese had been pushing gradually down to the coast of Africa. They mainly sought slaves and gold, but they also learned a great deal about deepwater navigation and the winds and currents in the Atlantic. A distant objective to all of their exploration was getting around the Cape of Good Hope and getting into the Indian Ocean where spices could be obtained.

A few years after Columbus's famous voyage, a small fleet commanded by Da Gama made it into the Indian Ocean and returned with a valuable cargo of spices. The Portuguese proceeded to develop this new market by sending regular fleets out. While doing so they established two precedents for the French, the Dutch, and the English who later followed them. In the first place, they did not develop significant colonial holdings. They merely established fortified trading posts, some like Goa, quite sizable. They had these posts along the coast of Africa as well as in the Indian Ocean. Brazil was, of course, an exception which will be discussed later.

A further, and in a way more important precedent, was a series of naval victories. Over the next 200 years, the European fleets in the Indies almost always beat native forces at sea. The apparent reason for this was that the large ships designed for the Atlantic could carry a broadside which gave them a great military value. The smaller and lighter ships used by the natives in the Indian Ocean could not withstand their gunnery. Why the Turks who had sizeable warships in their Mediterranean fleet did not build similar ships for the Indian Ocean is obscure. Even in the Mediterranean, their fleet never was fully rebuilt after Lepanto.

It's of some interest that 50 years before the arrival of the Portuguese, the Chinese had been moving very large ships into the Indian Ocean. The ships did not carry broadsides, but could easily have been reequipped. For purely domestic reasons, the Chinese stopped this exploration and indeed, made the construction of large ships illegal. Thus, the Europeans had in essence a monopoly of powerful ships in the Indian Ocean. They exploited it mainly for trading purposes, rather than sizeable colonies. There was a little Portugese settlement in Southern Africa in what eventually became Angola and Mozambique, and the Dutch landed a few farmers in South Africa. In these areas, tropical diseases were less dangerous than nearer the equator. Why this restraint is unknown to me, I hope some of my readers can solve the problem.

The Dutch, the leading naval power in the early years, seized several small islands where particular spices were grown. Their settlement around Batavia was somewhat larger than a simple trading post like those maintained by the other maritime powers.

Portuguese ships going far west in order to get around the bulge of Africa accidentally discovered Brazil. Here, instead of simply establishing trading posts, they began agricultural development, mainly using slaves imported from their African posts. They produced sugar and exported the bulk of it to Europe. For a while, it was a very prosperous colony, prosperous enough to attract Dutch aggression. The Dutch temporarily held much of the northern part of the Portuguese settlements. They were, however, driven out. The Portuguese did not get very far inland in Brazil and indeed, the Amazon basin is still largely undeveloped.

Note the rather odd situation. With the exception of the far south of Africa where the Dutch and the Portugese established small groups of farmers, only trading posts were established along the African coast and in the lands around the Indian Ocean. The Portuguese, however, settled on the western coast of the South Atlantic if not on the eastern coast. The Spaniards also had large settlements in the Americas. The only significant settlement in the Far East for a long time was the Spanish occupation of the Philippines. This was a rather accidental byproduct of Magellan's trip around the world. In the northern Philippines, the natives were brought under control and learned to speak Spanish and became Catholics.

Although not an important source of spices, the Philippines did export cinnamon. Manila was mainly important for trade with China, and was treated as rather an annex to Mexico. In spite of the vast distance across Pacific, an annual ship went from Manila to Acupulco. The Philippines were thus treated as a westward expansion of Spain's American holdings.

In the southern islands, the Moros were not successfully subjugated, and they began a war which, on a small scale, continues to this day. Guerrillas are hard to pacify. The northern Philippines was Hispanisized successfully, but not the southern. When the Spaniards, conquered the islands they were able to put down guerilla war in the northern Philippines, but not really eliminate it in the south. They were able to reduce it to a very small scale, but it continued under the independent Philippines government. The U.S. Army had a small advisory mission to help the Filipinos in this tiny war, but so far they have not extinguished it.

The Spanish possessions on the American continent were more or less the areas that today speak Spanish. The Spanish, like the Portuguese, made little effort to settle at the Amazon basin. Those parts of Peru, Columbia, etc. which are in the Amazon basin were left largely undeveloped and still are. Spanish explorers pushed north of the Mexican settlements and occupied what is now Florida. They also tried to establish a settlement in the Carolinas. The latter failed.

The small islands in the Caribbean could be used to raise sugar using imported black slaves. The business was extremely deadly, with 50% death rates from tropical diseases both for the slaves and their white supervisors. Nevertheless, these islands were thought to be the most valuable of the European colonial possessions and the newly developing naval powers of northern Europe, the Dutch, the French, and the English, fought among themselves and with Spain for them. From the perspective of the present day, this looks odd, but these small islands remained important and were the subject of major military campaigns right into the 19th-century.

The new northern naval powers began settling north of the Florida, holdings of Spain about 100 years after Columbus. Working from the North down, the English began trading for furs in the Hudson Bay very early. The Hudson Bay Company is still in existence and runs a chain of department stores in Canada. The French settled in what is now Québec about as early. They also were deeply interested in fur trading, but Québec is better for agriculture than a Hudson Bay area, and they began farming very early. The French had a very active missionary campaign which accompanied by fur traders, reached the end of the Great Lakes, crossed the easy portage to the Mississippi and finally reached the Gulf of Mexico. The French Catholic Church was very much interested in missionary activity and this might be one reason that, on the whole, the French had less trouble with the Indians than the English did farther south.

The area between the St. Lawrence and the Spanish settlements in Florida attracted settlement from a number of northern powers.

To take two minor ones, the Dutch founded New York, under another name naturally, and there was a Swedish colony in what is now New Jersey. The English captured New York and they had their own settlements beginning with Virginia which was settled for commercial reasons. They raised tobacco and on the whole, they were prosperous, although King James, who was 300 years ahead of the doctors in believing that smoking was dangerous, hindered its development.

The New England settlements were essentially religious although they also planned on farming. They attracted many settlers for religious reasons. The development of these colonies was very slow, partly, because of wars with the Indians. Only a few people wanted to move across the Atlantic. Criminals in England were frequently shipped across to temporary slavery in the Americas by the Captain of the ship, and free individuals could purchase their ship ticket by promising to permit themselves to be sold as a slave for a period of years. A good many slaves were brought in from Africa. Still the colonies did develop, and by the time of the Revolution, there were almost half as many people living in the English-speaking colonies as in the home country itself. A good many of them, of course, were slaves from Africa.

The individual colonies had governments which were small-scale copies of the British government. There was a royally appointed governor in much the same position as a king, his council which served much like the House of Lords, and an elected lower house.

The individual colonies were separately governed and indeed, travel between them was frequently harder than taking ships across the Atlantic to England.

Adam Smith was a professor of philosophy and felt that political philosophy was part of his field of expertise. He finished off the Wealth of Nations while what he refers to as "the late disturbances in the colonies" were underway. He devotes some space to the situation in the colonies and his suggestions for remedies. Other discussion which shows that he was generally familiar with the economic situation of the colonies is scattered through the book.

It is not absolutely clear in his very brief remarks, but Smith hoped that the colonies would be given suitable representation in London. Apparently, his idea was that they would send a number of representatives, perhaps 50, to the House of Commons, although the details were not developed. This was during the period of the rotten boroughs. Many of the seats in the House were owned by wealthy people who sat in the House of Lords. The introduction of a significant number of colonial representatives would have sharply reduced the value of these seats which had been purchased by people like, for example, the Pitt family. The proposal was never seriously discussed, but it would have run into difficulties with the powers that be if it had been attempted.

In this, as in many other areas, Smith's advice was good. It seems likely if it had been adopted when he was beginning his book, it would have prevented the Revolution. By the time his book was printed, a good deal of water had passed over the dam. The Continental Congress was in existence, fighting around Boston had developed, and the non-importation agreement had been implemented. Still, it is quite possible that the unification of England and its colonies could still have been successfully carried out.

As evidence of this possibility, consider Canada. In the seven-years war, it had been taken by England and they had established a standard colonial government modeled on the other ones in what became the United States. The French inhabitants objected and the House of Commons modified the government of Québec to be more in accord with French ideas. As a result, during the Revolutionary war, when a military force was sent to Québec by the Continental Congress, it was beaten off and Canada remained part of the British Empire. It seems likely that a similar attention to the views of the 13 colonies would have had much the same result.

The United States might, therefore, have had their capital in London for a number of years. Smith thought, that with the growing population on the western side of the Atlantic, it was likely that the royal capital would be moved across. Perhaps, it would go to Philadelphia or, as the west was developed, Pittsburg or Chicago. Personally, I wish his advice had been followed. A major government with a purely decorative king, taking in the United States, Canada, and the British Isles would have dominated the world even more than the present United States.[3]

---

[3] The rest of the British Empire might have been kept intact. The English-speaking colonies of Australia and New Zealand were not in existence then, but might have developed almost as rapidly as they did even if there were no prisons built in Australia.

It should be kept in mind that about the time the Declaration of Independence was signed, a scotch instrument repairman filed a patent for a steam engine with a separate condenser. A textile industry using machinery had already begun in England. The Industrial Revolution was underway and for the first few years, it was almost entirely an English operation. The Americans eventually overtook them, but an integrated Empire would have even more surely dominated the world, and might have prevented those great catastrophes, World War I and World War II. The British abolished slavery in their Empire in the early 19th-century without any bloodshed, albeit with higher taxes. Perhaps if America had not become independent, this would have extended to it, thus preventing that other great catastrophe, the civil war.

But this, of course, is a dream of what might have been. I shall continue with the practice of occasionally presenting such dreams for the reader's contemplation. We should always keep in mind that history might have gone differently and that this might have been either much better or much worse than what actually happened.

Chapter 3

The Balance of Power and The Revolution

The balance of power is sometimes referred to as a method of assuring peace. This could hardly be more wrong. The balance of power by preventing one country from becoming all powerful guarantees wars. The currently peaceful state, in the sense that there are no major wars, although continual minor wars, is an indication that the balance of power no longer controls international relations. The United States is the dominant power and there is no one at the moment who can balance them. On the whole, this situation is desirable although how long it will last is uncertain. The long series of minor wars, many of which are between the United States and a third- or even fourth-rate power, seem odd under the circumstances, but before I deal with that, I would like to describe the classical balance of power and its influence on the revolution.

With the collapse of the Roman Empire, Europe was broken into a number of small states. They were never reunited. Charlemagne, Napoleon, and Hitler each brought a large part of the Western European area under one control, but in no case did they control the entire former Roman Empire. There was of course the "unHoly, unRoman and unEmpire", but even disregarding its internal weakness, it covered only a small part of the former Roman Empire.

Why was the Roman Empire not put back together? The answer is the balance of power. Although leaders of states in Europe acted in accord with the balance of power for a thousand years, the modern theoretical discussion of it came from Hume many years after it had begun operating. Hume pointed out that when one state began to become powerful, other states would tend to ally with each other to protect themselves. Rome had overcome this in its wars with the Carthaginians, the Greek states successor to Alexander, and the barbarian states to their north and west. After Rome fell, no one was able to repeat it.

There is a remarkable difference between the history of Europe and that of China. Traditional China is about the same size as the Western European area controlled by Rome. Its history is one of uniting in a single dynasty, beginning in 221 B.C. but these dynasties normally lasted only 200–300 years. They would then decay and fall apart. After an interval of chaos, a new dynasty would come along which would reunite the entire area. The new dynasties might be native or one of the foreign conquest dynasties.

The last one, Ching, was a barbarian dynasty, the royal family of which continued to speak a nonchinese language among themselves. It formally ended in 1911, and there followed the historically normal civil war of the warlords with local officials, generals, and bandits attempting to establish a new dynasty. A strong central government was in fact reestablished in 1950 although its history since then raised a number of doubts as to whether it would be around for the 200–300 years of the standard dynasty.

Why the difference in the history of China and Europe? They're both big areas headed by many people who do not speak the same language. A Cantonese cannot easily understand a native of Peking. Of course, the written language is nonalphabetic and understood throughout the Empire. Unfortunately learning it is so difficult that not everyone could read and write. Still it must be admitted that the fact that officials in the capital could communicate in writing to scholars living on the borders of Tibet might have been one factor in getting the country to reunite whenever it broke apart. On the other hand, Europe had a somewhat similar situation when all educated people wrote in Latin.

Another possible explanation mentioned above is that China is a hydraulic state heavily dependent on irrigation canals. These canals were also used for transportation. This means the communications between different parts of China were easier than between say, Paris and Madrid. Large armies could be moved much more readily in much of China than in Europe north of the Mediterranean. Indeed, the decisive battle which established Ming as a ruling dynasty was a naval battle fought on an inland lake with the military forces being brought into action by way of canals. If the reader feels that neither of these explanations is decisive, so does the author. I would be delighted with suggestions of another explanation.

So far as I know, there were no other places where large scale and long lasting governments were established. If Alexander had lived even a few years longer, he might have established a Greek Empire. When he died, however, his generals immediately split the Empire and fought among themselves. The Arab Empire began disintegration fairly quickly because of dynastic squabbles. When the Turks seized a large part of the former Arab Empire, it split up also. Genghis Khan's Empire, history's largest, fell apart because of quarrels among his heirs.

India was never really united until the British came along. The Great Moguls, who had a large Indian empire, were unable to establish control over the whole of India that lasted more than the lifespan of one ruler.

At the end of the 14th-century, Spanish and Portuguese navigators opened up a new area for expansion. After Columbus, the Spaniards seized quite large areas of land in the Western Hemisphere. The areas they held can be readily identified, because they still speak Spanish. Why they did not occupy even larger areas is rather mysterious. To repeat, they also held the Philippines as an accidental byproduct of Magellan's circumnavigation. It was treated as a sort of annex to Mexico with an annual ship to Acapulco.

The restrictions on Portuguese settlement are equally mysterious. As a result of a navigation error, they found Brazil and settled the coastal area where they raised sugar with the help of slaves imported from Africa. Like the Spanish, they did not penetrate seriously into the Amazon basin. On the other side of the Atlantic, however, the Portuguese established a number of trading posts but no true colonies along the coast of Africa and on the shores of the Indian Ocean.

Notably, when other marine powers, the Dutch, the English, and the French also went around the Cape of Good Hope, they followed the same policy east of the Pope's line of trading posts rather than colonies for the first 200 years. Why sizeable colonies were established on the western shores of the Atlantic, but not on the eastern is not obvious. Eventually, near the southern tip of Africa, the Dutch and the Portuguese established small agricultural colonies.

A long chain of farming colonies was established along the Atlantic coast of the United States and Canada. At first they were fairly small, but by 1770 there were almost half as many Englishmen living on the western side of the Atlantic as in their homeland.

The balance of power did not seem to affect these more distant colonies until the middle of the 18th-century. In what we call the French-and-Indian war, and Europe calls it the seven-years war,[4] England took on almost all of the other countries in Europe and won thus establishing itself as the leading power and upsetting the balance of power.

It occurred to the new French Foreign Minister, Vergennes, that if the American colonies could be split off from England, England would be weaker and hence, the balance of power would be restored. Since the United States owe their independence to his action along these lines, they should be permanently grateful to him.

In that same seven-years war, Clive had won his great victory at Plassey and acquired a full province in India as a result. With that as

---

[4] It was actually started by George Washington, then a lieutenant colonel in the Virginia militia.

a start, England took the rest of India and many other colonies during the 19th-century. Her example was followed by France, Belgium, the Netherlands, and a late comer, Germany. Note that all these imperial powers were democracies by the standards of the time. The early economists thought that these colonies were worth less than their cost. Most modern economists think the same. In any event, the 19th-century was devoted to picking up real estate all over the world.

After World War II, almost all these lands were given up. In some cases, there was a native revolt, but in most cases, the withdrawal was voluntary. The Independence of the Indian peninsula was followed by a blood bath in which something like 1,000,000 people died. It was, however, inter-communal rioting rather than a war for independence. It's hard to think of rational reasons for this creation of big Empires and then their abandonment.

Turning to the balance of power, however, a political genius Bismarck was able to unite Germany into one country which was really too big for the European balance of power at that time. If Bismarck had been succeeded by other statesmen of equivalent political talent, it is likely that the balance of power would have been permanently upset. As it happened, however, he was followed by people of less ability and Germany failed to unite Europe.

While all of this was going on, the United States was gradually, in a series of small aggressive wars, conquering the Indian tribes that held most of the territory, now called the United States. As a result of this conquest, the United States was potentially the major power in the world although it showed no signs of wanting conquest and expansion once the Indians had been dealt with.

A quick and minor war with Spain introduced the United States into the great power league. Meanwhile, the balance of power was partially upset in Europe, because of the strength of Germany. This led to the two world wars and at the end of the second, the United States was probably the world's leading power, although Russia was in position to challenge that. Russia, however, fell apart with the result the United States is now unquestionably the most powerful nation in the world. There are, however, two very large nations, India and China, which are growing rapidly and may in another few decades get into position to challenge the United States.

The balance of power had prevented the development of a single over powerful state, and the creation of the United States and the weakness of the other countries meant that the balance of power is gone. Note that this weakness of the other states is largely voluntary and in a way a further legacy of Bismarck. Bismarck introduced the welfare state and the other major European countries followed his example.

The cost of the welfare state is very great and its political attractiveness in a democracy is also great. None of the European former great powers feels capable of both supporting the welfare state and a major military machine. In consequence, the former great powers in Europe all have relatively minor military machines. The United States, for example, has more carriers than the combined navies of Europe, and their position on land and in the air is roughly equivalent.

The situation looked quite different during World War II. Schumpeter said the war was three sided. Ignoring, as he did, the Japanese theater, that is correct. The United States, however, showed no signs of realizing that it had two potential opponents, Germany and Russia. The end product was that although undeniably Germany lost and Russia won, it's hard to say that the United States won the war. The eventual collapse of Russia, of course, put the United States in a dominant position.

It is noticeable that the Americans have made little gain out of their dominant position. They have been involved in three minor but bloody wars, and gained little from any of them. They are currently in a fourth. In the Korean War, fought before the collapse of Russia, the Americans marched to the Yalu, were outflanked and fell back in disarray.[5] The United States were able to put their force back together and march north almost to the prewar line of demarcation. They stopped there, apparently because the military did not think they had the power to firmly defeat the opponent. They certainly did not aim for unconditional surrender. Although they could have easily expanded their forces, they settled for an uneasy truce instead.

The same can be said about the Vietnam War. As the result of domestic difficulties in the United States, their forces were withdrawn from Vietnam and then, Congress cut off the ammunition supply for the Vietnamese army. In consequence, the Communist won and there was the usual Communist bloodbath.

---

[5] I was in the American Embassy during the later part of this war.

About two million people were killed in Cambodia and about 1,500,000 boat people died. This was a Communist country after all, and it can assume the secret police behaved as Communist secret police normally do, so there probably were many other casualties which were not made public. It is, however, forbidden to speak about it and the bulk of those Americans who fought so hard for the North Vietnamese in Chicago have refused to even think about it. The commander of the Vietnamese army said that they beat the French in Paris and United States in Chicago. That is correct.

Ironically, and even more unpleasant from the standpoint of the left which supported the north in Chicago and other cities, the new Vietnam is a very successful capitalist dictatorship. The American left fought for Democratic Socialism and these left-wing sources now refuse to even mention their disappointment. The flourishing state of capitalism and dictatorship in Vietnam should irritate them, but apparently does not. There is even a sort of implicit censorship in which the Vietnam outcome is not supposed to be even mentioned in discussions of the current Iraqi war.

At the moment, the Americans are in another very minor war. In spite of the tendency of the press to play up their casualties, they are actually very light, well under the number of people who die on their roads. But although the casualties are light, they show no signs of terminating. It is one of the old-fashioned wars of pacification which all of the colonial powers had in their empires. The Americans had similar difficulties with the Indians. History indicates that these things gradually die out, but that may be a long, long time off. Like the Vietnam War, it may be ended by a collapse of morale on their home front.

Meanwhile, the debris of the rest of the empires is unpleasant. Western Sudan is the worst of them, but many places in Africa are now much worse off than they were when they were governed by the European powers. In view of the voluntary military weakness of the European countries, it seems unlikely the empires will be reestablished. American policy in the area is almost nonexistent. Let's hope that these places will become peaceful and democratic, but that is a hope not a plan.

Altogether the end of the balance of power has left the world in a rather bad shape. It would be within the Americans power to act as a policeman for the backward parts of the world, but in view of the rather incoherent state of public opinion, I doubt, they would be very effective. This would not be because of their weakness, but because of a lack of clear cut objectives and methods of achieving them.

But what should the United States do? They are more powerful than any other country and probably more powerful then any two or three other countries. On the other hand, nuclear weapons are now widespread. Exactly the number of countries that could deliver one and destroy one of the U.S. major cities is unknown. It is considerable. Their present situation then, is far from ideal.

Long, long ago, in 1946, like Bertrand Russell, I was in favor of an immediate nuclear attack on the Soviet Union. Retrospectively, I wish it had been done. Everyone would have a longer life expectancy if we did not have to worry about some minor dictator killing us. On the other hand, at the time I was merely a law student, and so far as I know Russell's and my desires in this area were unique. I suspect that most of my readers feel that the decision not to eliminate the Soviet Union early was better than my desire to get rid of them.

Leaving that dream aside, what has been the U.S. foreign policy since 1945. They have been engaged in four minor wars, one of which is still going on, and cannot claim[6] that they gained anything much from them. On the other hand, their casualties were not excessive. To repeat, they lose many more lives on the roads in the average year than their military casualties.

In addition, there were a number of very small military operations. The Americans invaded Panama, Grenada, and briefly Haiti. They dropped a few bombs on former Yugoslavia, and there were a number of other trivial clashes between their forces and various other countries. None of them seemed to lead to any positive results. On the other hand, they suffered practically no casualties.

In general, in my opinion, the Department of the State thinks that meeting at the UN with other countries, giving speeches and listening to speeches by representatives of other countries, is a major accomplishment of the U.S. foreign policy. Nevertheless, their rigid unwillingness to let their citizens be subject to the unlimited jurisdiction

---

[6] I count Iraq and Afghanistan as one war. The present unpleasantness is the U.S. second attack on Iraq. They won the first quickly and easily.

of a world court seems to indicate a lack of confidence in the new international institutions. Putting it frankly, I can see no reason to believe that the U.S. foreign policy has accomplished much since World War II. On the other hand, I have not anything very much in the way of suggestions for activity. Perhaps, someone among my readers can fill the gap.

Chapter 4

The Revolutionary War

Putting the discussion of the Revolutionary war right after the balance of power is very suitable because the balance of power was heavily involved in the war of the American Revolution. The seven-years war had reduced the power of France so that it was no longer the first power in Europe, England was. France was unable to protect their long-lasting ally in eastern Europe, Poland, which was barbecued by its three neighbors. In spite of their long alliance with Turkey, they were unable to prevent the Russians from taking much of the Ukraine from them. Their colonial holdings had also been sharply cut back. In an exhibition of bad manners, England insisted that the British ambassadors to the European courts had ceremonial priority over the French.

The new French Foreign Minister, Vergennes was interested in a way of humbling England. Promoting independence for those English colonies on the western side of the Atlantic looked promising. An agent was sent for the purpose both of collecting information and perhaps stirring things up. Shortly, arms and money were provided to the Colonial militia through, oddly enough, the author of the Barber of Seville. The traditional ally of France, Spain collaborated in the arms provision. The Spanish cooperation was less than wholehearted, partly, because of the inefficiency of the Spanish Bourbons, and partly, because they feared that the independence movement might spread to the Spanish Americas.

Vergennes was deeply discouraged and might have given up after Washington's defeat at Long Island. General Gage's victory at Saratoga, however, restored Vergennes' morale and France formally declared war and sent a small expeditionary force to assist Washington. A major naval force was sent to the Caribbean and a smaller naval force, commanded by the only French admiral that the great naval historian and theorist, Mahan, really approved of was sent to the Indian Ocean. There were three significant naval battles in the Indian Ocean, which are normally ignored in the histories of the Revolutionary war.

Let me here interrupt my main narrative to deal with Washington's generalship, and then with the general problem of naval war under sail. It is generally said that Washington was a poor tactician, but a brilliant strategist. For the benefit of those of my readers who are unfamiliar with military theory, tactics is the art of winning battles, and strategy the art of using battles, and other operations to win wars. A good general is adept in both, but Washington was a poor tactician who lost most of his pitched battles, but he understood grand strategy so the Americans won the war.

The small, one might even call them tiny, victories at Princeton and Trenton were of major strategic importance even if they were very small. The British realized that in order to put down the rebellion, it was necessary to pacify the countryside. This meant a number of small garrisons scattered through the farming regions. Washington realizing that the small garrisons in Princeton and Trenton were indeed small, took his army across the Delaware to attack them. He was, of course, successful. The British had to give up the posting of small garrisons around the countryside, hence giving up the control of the country outside major cities to the Americans.

After Princeton, a long series of minor battles was fought in northern New Jersey. The British garrison in New York required forage for its horses, and sent out small parties to buy it. The farmers were apparently quite willing to sell, but Washington saw this as an opportunity to deal with small parties of British soldiers. The result was that in what is called the "forage war", vigorously fought, but not very large skirmishes were fought in northern New Jersey. Washington did not succeed in starving the horses of the British force, but on the whole the American troops did well.

It is necessary at this time to talk a little bit about the cold winter in Yorktown. Washington by now had realized that direct fighting with large British army forces was probably unwise. The British moved to Philadelphia, Washington followed and built an entrenched camp at Yorktown. Howe was probably convinced he could beat the Continental Army in the field, but attacking an entrenched army, particularly in the winter, was a much more difficult task. Perhaps had he stayed in Philadelphia through the summer, he might have tried then. The entrance of the French into the war, however, led the British government to order him to move back to New York. He did, winning a minor battle with Washington en route.

The French sent a small army to cooperate with Washington. The British were for a considerable time concentrated in New York with Washington and the French on guard nearby. Howe's forces were not sufficient to drive the combined armies away and the combined Americans and French were not strong enough to seize New York. The British thought that they would have more popular support in the South and Cornwallis with a small army was shipped south where he fought several minor battles, but was never able to establish control of the countryside. His independent cavalry force was wiped out at Green Mountain.

He marched north, forcing Jefferson to flee from his capital in Virginia, and reached Yorktown. It should be pointed out that he probably did not feel he was in any danger. A British general in possession of a port could normally wait there peacefully until the Royal Navy either reinforced or evacuated him.

Washington's fine strategic sense, however, came into play here. He arranged for De Grasse to bring the French Caribbean fleet up to blockade Yorktown. The French and American forces around New York evaded the British forces there and marched south for Yorktown. The march was peaceful except that the American troops, who had not been paid, refused to continue until they were paid. The French paid them.

The British naval forces in American waters, which were weaker than De Grasse, came down to help Cornwallis. There was a brief and not particularly bloody naval battle, and Graves withdrew. This minor engagement, called the battle of the Virginia Capes, should be listed as one of the decisive battles of history, but so far as I know it is not.

Cornwallis had no alternative, but to surrender and his surrender convinced the English government that they could not win back the Colonies. Meanwhile, however, De Grasse had gone back to the Caribbean and continued with his policy of reconquering islands from the British.

Here I must take a further brief detour to talk about naval warfare in the days of sail. The British and French had quite different ideas about strategies and tactics at sea. In order to understand them, it is necessary to turn to the theoretical work of Alfred Thayer Mahan, the great naval historian. Ships depending on the wind could run down wind easily, but had to engage in the tedious work of tacking to go up wind. There was also another technical difference here. If you were sailing across the wind, perhaps as part of a tacking maneuver, or simply because that was the direction you wished to go, the wind would make your ship lean away. This would mean that your broadside cannon on the up wind side would be automatically elevated which would give them longer-range. Ships on the windward would lean also, but their guns would be depressed and hence have shorter range.

In maneuvering for position before engaging the French usually tried to get downwind and the English sought the weather gage, or in more modern language, up wind. Thus as a general rule the English were in a position to decide whether or not there would be an engagement. The French were willing to put up with this, because they normally had an "ulterior' objective. They weren't aiming to fight the English at sea, but to seize some piece of real estate, an island, for example, and didn't want a battle to interfere with their operations.

The English, on the other hand, thought of winning battles as the principal objective of naval operations and sought out battle when they were superior. When they were inferior, they normally attempted to combine with another English fleet. As a result, when there was a battle, the English normally won. Trafalgar will do as an example. The combined French and Spanish fleets out numbered the British, but Nelson attacked . Further, the most powerful warship afloat, the Spanish Sanctisima Trinidad was part of the allied forces. Villeneuve apparently lost his head. He failed to order the leading ships of his line to join the battle. They eventually did on their own initiative, but it was too late.

I now close my digression on the problems of naval warfare under sail. If the reader is curious, he may turn to the many volumes written by Alfred Thayer Mahan on the subject. From the standpoint of general history, this is an important matter, but it can be left to the brief treatment given above for the purposes of this particular history.

Turning to the history itself, when he left Yorktown, De Grasse continued his campaign of seizing islands in the Caribbean. At one point, he found himself in contact with Rodney's fleet in a position where his fleet was more powerful and up wind of the British. In addition, there was an island behind the British and they could not withdraw. De Grasse ignored them and continued in the direction of his ulterior island objective. During the night, Rodney was reinforced. This led to the battle of the Saints which was a great English victory. It did not mean that England won the war, but it did mean that they had a face-saving way of getting out of the war. They took it and the U.S. became independent.

Chapter 5

Early Policy, Looking East

When Washington became President, the United States was essentially a thin chain of settlements along the Atlantic Coast from Maine to South Carolina. The U.S. pre-1890 foreign policy in general fits nicely into two categories; dealing with the Atlantic, and dealing with the interior.

I will start with the Atlantic. The Americans had no real Navy, although privateers had played a significant role in the Revolution and the French had provided them with one ship which won a battle with the English. The Continental Congress which had been the sole government before the establishment of the constitution, had not had funds to do much about this. Washington at first also did not build a significant Navy.

The Revolution was in fact a world war with France and Spain, with some assistance from other European countries, attempting to humble England which had won the seven-years war. They thought that the splitting off of the American colonies would mean that about a third of all Englishmen would become independent and hence England would be weaker. Thus, they provided the Americans with arms and ammunition, and financial support. They declared war on England when the American forces at Saratoga demonstrated that they could win a battle against England.

Most of the fighting, however, was carried on by French and Spanish forces and it was mainly a naval war. As I mentioned earlier, there were three major naval battles in the Indian Ocean between French and English ships. The final battle which marked the end of the war was the naval battle mentioned above in the Caribbean which the English won although they cannot be said to have won the war. Florida and Minorca, captured by England in the last war, went back to Spain.

Very shortly, the French Revolution broke out and led to another war between France and England which involved the whole continent of Europe before Napoleon was beaten at Waterloo. The French privateers brought some of their captures into American ports for sale. Since the English objected, this led to a serious foreign policy problem which Washington was able to prevent from leading to war.

The United States built a small navy of frigates. They were somewhat larger than the standard frigate in use in the traditional navies and, as a result of improved hull design, somewhat faster. This led to their beating several French frigates in a small undeclared war which the U.S. had with the French who objected to them for not cooperating with their privateers. Since the French Navy was much weaker than the English navy, however, this was not a long-lasting or even very serious war.

The English manned their Navy by impressment, which differed very little from kidnapping. Most of the common sailors on their ships had been seized by press gangs and had to be carefully guarded by marines to prevent their escape. In addition, they would stop ships, including the American ships, inspect the crew, and claim that some among them were deserters from the Royal Navy. Modern historians believe that such deserters were reasonably frequent on American merchant ships and perhaps, naval ships. It is dubious, however, that the British naval captains were either very good at, or highly motivated to try, separating genuine American citizens from naval deserters.

Two different methods dealing with this problem were adopted by the American first Presidents. In the first place, a building program with frigates and six genuine ships of the line was put in hand by Adams. In addition, Jay was sent to England to negotiate a treaty on the impressments matter. He succeeded in getting a treaty under which the American government would provide certificates to ships which had been searched by American government officials. The certificates would insure that there were no deserters from the Royal Navy aboard. For reasons that are unclear, this was met with considerable indignation in the American press. Its negotiation was not completed until the end of Adams administration and Jefferson did not even send it to the Senate for ratification.

In 1800, Jefferson replaced Adams as President.[7] Jefferson stopped construction of the ships of the line to save money. He spent part of the money saved by an immensely wasteful effort to build five canals across the Appalachians. This was beyond the engineering skills of that day, hence they were not completed. This was a particularly important mistake. In the war of 1812, the British thought that the partially built ships of the line were important enough so that they put landing parties ashore and burned all of them in their stocks in order to make sure they were not completed.

As a digression, what would have happened if they had been completed. They would have been ready at the time of Trafalgar, and might have been enough to change the outcome. Whether they actually would have been enough, whether they would have been committed, and last but not least, whether this would have been to an advantage, are all subjects of amusing speculations.

The frigates were sent to war against Tripoli. The Tripoli Navy actually engaged in piracy and the Americans were one of the victims. They were willing to stop if paid, but the Americans had a slogan "Millions for defense, not one cent for tribute". The frigates were sent off to Tripoli and engaged in a blockade and bombarding the city. Since most of the city was made of mud brick, and the artillery mainly fired solid cannon balls, the Dey of Tripoli was not much inconvenienced by the bombardment. The blockade no doubt inconvenienced

---

[7] Adams had more votes among those who actually voted than Jefferson, but the so-called "slave vote" elected Jefferson.

the Tripolitans, but their ships were mainly shallow draft, and the Americans deep draft frigates were unable to prevent them from getting in and out of harbor if they stayed close to the coast.

Due to the shallow water together with the absence of good charts, the Americans lost one frigate, the Philadelphia, which ran aground and was then taken by the Tripolitan Navy. This led to the only highly successful activity of the American Navy in this war. Decatur led a small party that succeeded in getting into the harbor, boarding the Philadelphia, and setting it afire.

In general, the American force was badly handled by a set of elderly Commodores. In the course of the circulation of these Commodores, one good Commodore, Preble, had command for a while. His principal accomplishment, however, was the training of captains for frigates who fought in the war of 1812.[8]

Meanwhile, an army officer with a few Marines[9] had picked up a contender to the throne of Tripoli and marched from Cairo towards that city. The American Navy apparently not wanting the army to win their war signed a very unfavorable peace treaty with the Dey. The Americans paid tribute. They also temporarily laid up the frigates. The money saved on the Navy was again thrown away in the unsuccessful effort to build five canals across the Appalachians.

---

[8] For a detailed but unimaginative account of the U.S. naval operations see: "Victory in Tripoli, Joshua E. London, Wiley, Hoboken, New Jersey. In spite of the title of the book, they lost the war.

[9] Hence, "To the Sands of Tripoli".

Meanwhile, France and England were at war and this imposed various inconveniences on the Americans. The impressment of their seamen was the one that caused the most noise. Since Jefferson had not only weakened the Navy to the point where it could have no effect, but also had cut back on the army, the Americans had little in the way of traditional tools which they could use. Jefferson then invented the embargo which has caused so much difficulty in the U.S. dealings with Cuba.

The refusal to engage in foreign trade with France and England had little effect on France, which was under English blockade. England, however, had been importing quite large amounts of food from the United States, and the effect on the poor or, at any event, the least well-off, was quite severe and caused political difficulties for the then British government. It is possible that it was one of the reasons that there was a temporary interruption in the war between England and France.

As an aside here, in general, the Federalists favored England and the Republicans, like Jefferson favored France. Eventually, of course, in 1812, the Americans would get into the war on France's side. Between the imposition of the embargo and the outbreak of the war, however, it seems likely that the major cost of the embargo fell on American shipping interests. They were mainly in New England and were Federalist in their voting pattern. In consequence, Jefferson and his successor, Madison, could easily withstand their suffering.

During the temporary truce between France and England, Napoleon arranged to have part of the Spanish empire in the New World,

Louisiana, transferred to France. Realizing that the war with England was starting again, and that he could not defend it against the British Navy, he suggested to Jefferson that it be sold to the United States for a very low price. Jefferson, although surprised by the offer, of course, agreed thus almost doubling the continental United States.

It should be said that Jefferson was mainly interested in opening the Mississippi River for American commerce. He had sent a mission to Paris to discuss the creation of a free trade area for American commerce near the mouth of the River. He was, to repeat, surprised when the French delegate, Talleyrand, suggested that he might wish to buy the entire Louisiana holding. To repeat again, this nearly doubled the United States, although with the exception of a few fur traders, the area was unoccupied by anyone except the Indians.

Since Jefferson was a large-scale slaveholder, and, further, his plantation was in an area that regularly bred slaves and exported them to the unhealthy deep South, it is not surprising that there was no provision in the annexation treaty which made the freeing of all slaves in the French empire by the early French Republican government continue to apply in Louisiana. It's of some interest that Jefferson's replacements as Democratic–Republican presidents were also slaveholders. The early states admitted to the union from the Louisiana Purchase were all slave states with the result that the constitutional protections for the "slave vote" became more important than they had been earlier.

Historical speculation is always fun although it is, of course, speculation. If the earlier French freeing of the slaves had been maintained in the Louisiana Purchase, there would have been fewer senators from slave states, fewer members of the Electoral College from the slave states and fewer slave states. This might have prevented the Civil War.

Since the Louisiana Purchase area was almost completely unknown, Jefferson found it necessary to send out an expedition to explore it. This expedition led Lewis and Clarke actually reached the Pacific coast. Except for some trading up the river from New Orleans and a certain amount of barge traffic by Americans, the Mississippi basin was largely empty of whites, and of course, the "purchased" areas west of that river were also.

Some Spanish ships had worked up the West Coast as far as the present Canadian border, but had not settled anywhere. The Catholic Church had done a certain amount of missionary work north of the settled area, but most of the churches and missions there today were built somewhat later.

The Louisiana territory purchased had as its eastern boundary, the Mississippi. Its western boundary was not at all clear and the Lewis and Clark expedition probably went beyond it. In any event, a good deal of what eventually became the states of Washington and Oregon was also claimed by England.[10,11]

---

[10] Bemis uses two maps to deal with the problem. The first on page 136 shows the situation and boundaries as they were understood at the time of the original purchase. The final boundaries of the area as determined by a treaty with Spain in 1817 are shown in another map on page 192.

[11] A Diplomatic History of the United States by Samuel Flagg Bemis, Henry Holt and Company, New York. This is an extremely detailed and long history. There have been many reprints. The one I have is the 1952 edition.

The principal differences are that Texas was retained by Spain, eventually, Mexico of course, and Oregon and Washington were eventually transferred. At the time of the original transfer, Napoleon was allied with Spain. A little later, Napoleon tried to impose a relative of his as king of Spain and most of the American Spanish possessions went into revolt. After 1815, the traditional dynasty was reestablished in Spain and temporarily in Mexico, but not in South America, and the Spanish ambassador to Washington maintained that the transfer was not legal, because the French did not own the area. He also said that, in any event, it covered only a thin strip along the Mississippi which was, of course, all that was known before the Lewis and Clarke expedition. Spain being by then, a very weak power, the Americans were able to ignore their objections. When Mexico became independent, it did not attempt to reach the boundaries Spain had claimed.

The impressment of the U.S. seamen continued. In 1812, partly for that reason, but, more importantly, because they wanted to annex Canada, the U.S. declared war on England. This was just as Napoleon, who would be their ally in that war, was marching on to Moscow. Obviously a very badly timed war and the Americans deserved to lose, as they did.

The frigates had been put back into a commission and some were able to sneak out of harbors in spite of the British blockade. On the whole, they did very well, being as has been mentioned before, larger than most British frigates, but they were merely an annoyance to the

British. The U.S. privateers in this war as in previous ones also did well, but again only an annoyance for the British. Mahan uses this short period of what he calls "Commerce War", as an evidence supporting his belief in a large navy.

The Americans efforts to conquer Canada failed completely. As an example of the poor quality of most of their military efforts, the American general in Detroit surrendered unconditionally to the British Commander on the opposite side of the border although the Americans outnumbered him about four to one.[12]

The border ran through several large lakes and small navies were built by both sides on the lakes. The Americans won two naval battles on the lakes, and put an expeditionary force ashore to burn York, the capital of Canada. The British later repaid this by burning Washington.

Meanwhile, Napoleon had been finished and the British sent an expeditionary force to Louisiana. The only clear-cut large-scale victory that the American army won in the war was Jackson's defeat of that British force. This, no doubt had much to do with his later distinguished career ending in the Presidency, but had no effect on anything else, because a peace had been signed in Europe three days before the battle was fought.

Altogether, the presidency of Jefferson and Madison were periods when the Americans failed in almost everything that they attempted

---

[12] 1812: The War that Forged a Nation by Walter Borneman, Harper, New York, 2004, is an excellent account of the fighting along the Canadian frontier and the extreme military ineptness of the U.S. forces. A very young commander, Scott, however, did do well. The end product was that the border remained more or less unchanged.

in foreign policy to their east. Fortunately, England was exhausted by her long fight with France. By Waterloo, the American population was much larger than it had been at the time of the Revolutionary war, and England decided not to attempt to reconquer it. In spite of Madison's general failure in the war, I suspect that he would have been able to defend the Americans against the exhausted English.

Chapter 6

1815 to 1890 to the East

From Waterloo to the Marne, the world was hardly peaceful, but the biggest wars were domestic. The Americans fought the largest war they ever had in terms of percent of population killed and damage to the economy over the issue of slavery. Two other very large domestic wars elsewhere are rarely covered much in American accounts of history. One was the Taiping rebellion in China, an immensely destructive war, probably much more destructive than the American Civil War. There was also the Indian mutiny which again is not covered much in American history books. Neither in the Taiping rebellion nor in the Mutiny were there good statistics on the damage or casualty rates, but the Americans do know that they were very major.

Jackson, who was in charge of the U.S. forces in the southwest, invaded the Spanish colony of Florida for the purpose of arresting and executing two Englishmen who were selling arms to the Indians. Since they were in Florida, a Spanish possession, this was quite legal, but Jackson objected. This led to trouble with Spain which was on the long down course from great power to minor nation. Monroe, then the Secretary of State succeeded in negotiating a purchase of Florida from Spain, thus ending the problem.

The Crimean war and the wars by which Germany and Italy were unified, involved major powers, but were much smaller in scale than either the wars of the French Revolution and Empire or the two world wars. The United States was not involved in either of these, not tremendously large wars.

There were many other minor wars. In the former Spanish empire in the Americas, there were a number of wars and almost innumerable revolutions. There was also a rather skilful American freebooter, Wallace, who was quite successful in Central America for a number of years. The expansion of the empires into Africa and Asia led to a number of minor wars. It's interesting that the expansionary countries were all, by the standards of the time, democracies. They were England, the biggest; France, second-biggest; but in their case a large part of their Empire was the Sahara Desert, the Netherlands, Belgium, and Germany. The latter a late arrival and hence, only a minor gainer, also grabbed "backward" countries. The Americans have a habit of announcing that their opponents in war were dictatorships and hence, did not recognize that Imperial Germany was as democratic as England.

This chapter deals only with the U.S. activities to their East, and they were not much engaged in any international wars during this period. There were a number of minor operations by the U.S. navy or Marines in various places which they regarded as backward.[13]

---

[13] See Boot "The Bloody Wars of Peace."

Perhaps as a result of the U.S. naval difficulties in the 1812 war, they built up their Navy, and by the 1840s had a respectable Navy although not, of course, capable of dealing with a major naval power. Between the 1840s and the Civil War, the Americans permitted their Navy to decline to some extent, but it was still powerful enough to blockade the Southern states.

Except for the civil war, the Navy really had no important duties during this period. The ships traveled all over the world and one frigate participated in the opium wars. This was the idea of its captain, who said: "blood is thicker than water" and joined in with the British in the bombardment of the Chinese forts. Communications between United States and North China were poor at that time and he received no orders.

This seems a good opportunity to discuss my combined source and competitor Samuel Flagg Bemis whose 809-page book "A Diplomatic History of the United States" covers the period from before the Revolution to the 50s.[14] The first 430-pages of this book deals with the time before the Spanish war. He discusses the Revolutionary war, the war of 1812, and the Mexican war in detail and with great competence. I have felt safe, therefore, to devote rather little space to these unimportant wars. The reader can turn to Bemis for an excellent and detailed account.

Probably the most important thing done by the U.S. Navy before the Civil War was the opening of Japan. This was a very well thought

---

[14] Henry Holt & Co, New York, 1952.

out and ingenious operation with no bloodshed. It seems likely, however, that England would have opened Japan a few years later if they had not.

The U.S. Navy was permitted to decline somewhat from about 1840 to the outbreak of the Civil War. It was, however, still strong to maintain a blockade of the South. This blockade caused continuing minor difficulties with England. England not only complained about the blockade, but also built two very strong but unarmored cruisers for the Confederates which successfully raided the U.S. international shipping. The U.S. Navy was mainly involved in the blockade, and hence there were only a few ships to protect their commercial ships. Their merchant marine was almost wiped out by the British built cruisers. Eventually, they paid substantial damages for the work of these cruisers.

The Americans blockade was by no means airtight. Some ships were able to get through and indeed, the Southern artillery was mainly equipped with English guns. In a way the principal sufferers from their blockade were not the Southerners, but the English workers who had been employed in the cotton textile industry. Fortunately, they were mainly politically opposed to slavery, and hence did not make any effort to push the British Navy to break the blockade.

Henry Adams, whose famous autobiography[15] covers this period, was the son of the American Ambassador in England, and points out that the upper classes in England were almost uniformly pro-confederate.

---

[15] The Education of Henry Adams.

Fortunately, the combination of the English working population favoring the North and the introduction of new technology in the form of armored warships which made the British Navy temporarily behind the times, meant that they did not enter the war in order to break the blockade.

The first naval battle of the war was Memphis, which was fought on the Mississippi River, far from the sea. Surprisingly, the ships on the Union side were actually parts of the army and not of the Navy. The Navy, however, quickly produced a river squadron which was a great help to Grant.

The blockade was further extended internally by Farragut. After having run the forts in the delta, he took New Orleans. He then ran some other forts upstream from New Orleans and spent many months in the waters of the Mississippi between those forts and the Confederate forts at Vicksburg. This internal extension of the blockade was most inconvenient to the Confederates. Farragut was supplied by rafts which were drifted down past the forts at Vicksburg. The failure of the Confederates to stop this at Vicksburg, was one further evidence of their naval incompetence. Farragut undoubtedly deserves the large park in his name in Washington.

After the Civil War, the U.S. Navy was permitted to decline sharply with ships sometimes being repaired by giving the shipyard another ship to junk. They also began a program of naming ships after Indian tribes. This led to the peculiar situation in which sailors frequently could not pronounce properly the name of their ship.

After a while, the Americans began rebuilding their Navy. Apparently, their motive was jealousy of Chile which was building a Navy in the South Pacific. The Navy that the U.S. built towards the end of the 19th-century, although a sizable improvement, was by no means a first-rate force. Before the Spanish-American war, many European observers thought the Spanish Navy was stronger. Since the U.S. won two naval victories, they were clearly wrong. But I'm putting that and the Spanish-American war off so I will not discuss it further here.

Chapter 7
West of the Appalachians, the Early Period

Compared to the Pyrenees or the Alps, the Appalachians is not a very large mountain range. They are, however, long and except for the Cumberland gap have no real opening through them. If the Americans had won the war of 1812 they could have got around the Appalachians to their North. Eventually, the Erie Canal just south of the Great Lakes opened an easy route to the West. This was, however, completed not very long before railroads became practicable. The engineering feat of the Erie Canal was outstanding, but it only speeded up settlement in the West by about 10 to 15 years.[16]

The original settlers in what became the United States were mainly east of the Appalachians, but the existence of good farmland to the West was well known. It was, of course, inhabited by Indians and they had more or less allied with the English during the Revolutionary war.

To say that they had allied implies more organization and strength for the Indian tribes than they actually had. Although there was the Iroquois federation in the North, that was only a loose union since it

---

[16] My great-grandfather took the Erie Canal on his way from Scotland to Illinois.

was primarily a hunting and gathering society and the population was very thin. To the South, similar hunting and gathering societies were even less organized.

The Indians got along badly with the few Americans who operated in their area. They also got along badly with each other, with most tribes being more or less at war with their neighbors. This was extended to the American settlers whenever possible.

When I lived in Blacksburg, Virginia, a neighboring small city put on a historical drama drawn from actual history to attract tourists. Indians from about 400 miles to the West raided the village and took off three women. The women finally escaped and succeeded in getting back to their families. This is simply one example of the kind of thing that went on pretty constantly. Of course, it should be kept in mind that the settlers also were uncomfortable neighbors. Mostly, however, they simply seized land and began farming. The Indians obviously objected, but over time the military strength of the settlers was usually greater than that of the Indians and hence, the frontier of settlement moved West in a series of fits and starts.

Mostly, the westward movement was little supported by the central government, such as it was. One minor war, west of the Appalachians, was aimed at the settlers, not the Indians. Hamilton had imposed a tax on distilled alcoholic beverages. Granted the almost nonexistence of roads across the Appalachians, whiskey was almost the only thing which was compact enough to carry to the East Coast for sale. The settlers refused to pay the tax and Washington organized a militia force to compel them. He went along personally in command and was able to get them to give in without significant bloodshed.

The only significant battle fought with the Indians in the area in the early years was Mad Anthony Wayne's victory at fallen timbers. In spite of his sobriquet, he fought a carefully planned and cautious battle, and won a well-deserved victory. In the treaty at the end of the Revolutionary war, the English had transferred the Ohio territory, the whole land area between the Ohio River and the Great Lakes and the east of the Mississippi, to the United States. They had, however, retained some forts there and provided supplies of various sorts to the Indians. After Wayne's victory and a demonstration at the nearby fort, they withdrew. After all, they needed to concentrate on France.

It may be sensible to interrupt the main course of my historical narrative to deal with the general problem of the Indians. Although some of the Indians on the East Coast were agricultural, and in fact taught the Americans to raise corn, mostly the Indians lived by hunting and gathering. Those that did engage in agriculture, except for the pueblos in the south west, farmed only a small part of their holdings, hunting in the rest. Granted their very small population, they were readily able to feed themselves.

It takes much more land to support a given number of Indians engaged in hunting and gathering or intermittent shifting agriculture, than to support a similar number of whites engaged in settled agriculture. Thus although the Indians were, in terms of their technology, in occupation of most of the United States, from the standpoint of farmers, it was more or less empty.

The desire of the farmers to take this apparently unused agricultural land is obvious. The objection of the natives unless they could be taught agriculture was equally obvious. American settlement plans in the West frequently involved efforts to teach the Indians to farm. Clark, of Lewis and Clark, was for a while more or less governor of much of the Louisiana Purchase. One of his continuing objectives was to teach the Indians to farm. Unfortunately, he was in general unsuccessful. The Indians wanted to continue using most of the land for hunting and gathering, even though this was immensely wasteful of real estate. The farmers wanted to take over what appeared to be prime farmland.

There was another major problem which was the fact that the Indians were a very belligerent group of people. Indeed, raiding their neighbors was regarded as both a pleasant and exciting occupation and a source of honor in their tribes. For obvious reasons, the farmers objected to this. Once there were a number of farmers in any area, complete with firearms, they could hold the Indians off. If, however, a potential farmer went out ahead of the frontier of settlement so that he would have first choice of land and hence would do well if he stayed alive, he was in danger. Such individual farmers were obvious targets of Indian raiding parties. The situation which moved gradually west with the frontier of settlement, led to a good deal of bloodshed.

Presumably there are records of all this in various county archives, but no one seems to have surveyed them fully. The forced transfer of the Cherokees from east to west attracted a good deal of attention from some missionaries who recorded it and called this the "Trail of Tears". Tocquiville happened to be in Wisconsin when a local tribe was driven across the Mississippi in the heart of the winter. Wisconsin winters are cold, but the Indians, living a hunting gathering life, probably were reasonably well equipped for life in the open. They had to go out from time to time to hunt for their food and hence probably had warm clothing.

The eastern states normally claimed parts of the area west of the Appalachians. They then distributed it to various economic interests, but when the people to whom they had distributed the land arrived would normally found squatters complete with muskets there. It should be pointed out that these were Americans and they set up local governments complete with elected sheriffs, juries, and County Clerks. Trying to expel these people would have been close to impossible. They were organized for war with the Indians and in many cases had what were called "private forts".

George Washington had received large grants of land west of the Appalachians and when he went out to inspect it after the Revolution, he found much of it occupied by squatters. It took him three years and a long and difficult lawsuit to get what was a small part of his holding back. He apparently gave up trying to get the rest of it. If Washington had this problem, you can imagine what a group of merchants from

Philadelphia who were attempting to develop land and had a grant from one of the eastern states which claimed sovereignty would face in an effort to establish their ownership. In general, they gave up.

This rather illegal process continued until 1862 when the Homestead Act made it possible for anyone to legally seize land for a farm. The interests of the Indians were mainly ignored in this legislation. Unfortunately, as you go West in the Great Plains, rainfall declines. Thus, the legally seized homesteads were sometimes too far west for really successful farming on 160 acres. Much of the land was better suited for larger acreages, or ranching, and difficulties between the farmers and ranchers formed part of the folklore of the frontier. Still, American agricultural communities, some of which were cattle raisers, pushed steadily west. Before the Civil War, dealing with the Indians was mainly done by militia. After the Civil War, regular army troops were involved. In both cases, however, the Indians were dispossessed and the Whites took over the land. In general, as I suppose is not surprising, there was much ill will between the Indians and the settlers.

The moral implication of this depends on which particular moral code you happen to believe in. My early training in the orient made me a moral relativist, so I shall not attempt to solve the moral problem here. I should point out, however, that one of the Americans early great writers, Washington Irvine, wrote a very attractive piece sympathizing with the Indians in which he hypothesized the man on the moon as one of the characters. Another of their great writers, Mark Twain who had spent much time in the West, attacked eastern intellectuals on the grounds that they did not actually know the Indians, and hence failed to realize the advantages of "civilizing" them. To repeat, I am a moral relativist and hence, merely note that both sides were behaving in accordance with their own moral code.

It should be emphasized that the United States is not alone in occupying territory which formerly was held by someone else. To take one very close parallel, China enters history as a series of settlements in the Yellow River Valley. It gradually expanded south apparently in much the same way as the United States expanded west. In both cases, the local population which was technically rather backward was shoved aside. In both cases, careful historical study is lacking. Nevertheless, Chicago and Canton are large cities in areas which were seized from their original inhabitants. In both cases also, there is little in the way of careful historical study of the matter and today nobody questions the right of the present occupants to the territory.

But leaving morals aside, the United States became the world's most prosperous and the most powerful country in the world as a result of seizing this land from the Indians. In a long series of minor aggressive wars, the Americans converted themselves from a thin strip of settlement along Atlantic into a continental power. They are now the world's leading power in both military and economic power. China is rapidly growing and may be their rival in military and economic power in the not distant future. Her historic right to southern China was much same as the Americans' right to the West. I should note that China and India are both large countries and are growing rapidly. In another 20 or 30 years, they may be in a position to rival them or for fighting along their poorly demarcated, disputed, and lengthy common border.

The Americans should, however, note another aggressive war, with Mexico. Settlers moving west from the southern part of United States settled in Texas, bringing their slaves with them. Although slavery was nominally illegal in Mexico, at first the Mexicans welcomed them and gave them title to their land. Mexico, however, was in that long series of revolutions, coups, and dictatorships which characterized its government after independence from Spain. Texans, not liking the system, revolted. After a campaign including the famous siege of the Alamo, the Mexican army was destroyed at the battle of San Jacinto.[17]

Not only was the Mexican army beaten but the President of Mexico was also taken prisoner and signed a more or less unconditional surrender. Texas immediately attempted to join the United States as a state, but was rejected. The details of the rejection were complicated but it seemed that slavery, at that time gradually becoming important, an issue might have been significant.

---

[17] The battle was interesting from the aspect of military history. Houston retreated before Santa Anna's forces almost all the way across Texas. He then turned and delivered a surprise attack directly at the center of the Mexican army in broad daylight across an open field. The Mexicans were on siesta.

Texas then made effort to establish itself as a nation, although this was always a second–best alternative to the Texans, who wanted to join the United States. They were not very successful in their efforts to join the Commonwealth of Nations, although at one point England and France recognized them. Eventually the United States permitted their entry. They naturally came in as a slave state. Like the other slave states in the southern part of Jefferson's Louisiana Purchase, their votes in the Senate and Electoral College were important in preserving slavery from legal elimination. When the war finally came, the Texans showed their fighting spirit and indeed only rejoined the union well after Lee's surrender.

The Indians residing in Texas and the other western states taken from Mexico in the same war did not recognize Mexican sovereignty and hence they did not recognize the transfer to the United States. They defended themselves as did the other Indians, and Geronimo, from that area, was probably the most determined Indian opponent in the western part of what became the United States.

The "war" went on until the Indians were finally subdued. Ironically, this left them scattered all over the United States in small reservations as well as some large ones. The individual institutions on these reservations vary a good deal, but many of them hold their land in common with the result that they suffer from the "tragedy of the Commons".

The Supreme Court of United States, in one of its more muddled decisions, made it possible for these reservations to set up gambling casinos. Thus the Indians, today, have rented out bits and pieces of their reservations for casinos, in some cases very profitably. I doubt the situation will continue indefinitely because I imagine the states will eventually let other people put up casinos. This process has begun along the great rivers. Still at the moment, the Indians are making a nice profit on a business which many American Protestants think is immoral and should be illegal.

The discovery of gold in California came at almost the same time as the Mexican war. There was an immediate rush of migrants to California, which developed rapidly. The Indian wars, however, continued and the immigrants who went overland normally traveled in big wagon trains which could circle the wagons and hence form a sort of fort if attacked by Indians. In other words, the war between the Americans and the Indians continued and the American successes also continued.

I have above mentioned the moral problem raised by this. In defense of the United States, I should point out that if the Indians learned to farm, and a good deal of effort was made by government officials to teach them, they could have occupied an adequate area for the purpose of raising crops. This would be only a part of their hunting range thus leaving plenty of land for both themselves and white settlers. They chose not to and the Indian problem has been with them now for many years. Fortunately, it is in general not much of a handicap to development.

I would like to discuss here the Monroe doctrine, which the reader may think should logically go into the discussion of foreign policy to the East, but I think it was a byproduct of our western policy. By 1820, the West was beginning to fill up and it was becoming obvious that in another war Canada, then as now a thin strip of settlement along the American border, was indefensible. This was a period when the great empires were built. England was the largest grabber of other people's property, but notably did not seize significant parts of South and Central America. They even defended the independent states in the Americas from other potential imperialists.

The explanation for this, I think, is a feeling on their part that the United States might object to seizure by the English of part of South America and take retaliation against Canada. They suggested to the United States a joint proclamation saying that the Latin American states should remain independent. The Americans decided to do it themselves, but they were not then really strong enough to prevent major European powers from seizing parts of South America. The English did protect the Latin American states from other imperialists, but, in my opinion, they were unable to extend their empire in that area themselves, because of the Americans' ability to retaliate on Canada.

But the reader may object to my explanation of the doctrine and where I have placed it in my book. There is also the fact that when the Americans were preoccupied by the civil war, the French established Maximilian as Emperor in Mexico. With the Northern victory, an army was sent to the Texan border, and the French withdrew. This was one case where the English did not need to defend the doctrine. As a result of the civil war, the Americans temporarily had a powerful army.

Certainly the English, for obvious reasons, never openly offered this explanation. I must admit my arguments for this are not terribly strong, but it seems to me that this is the most likely explanation. With the decline of England as a great power and the corresponding rise of the United States, the Americans became the main defender of the Doctrine.

Chapter 8

More on the West

The Indians however were not the Americans only rivals for land in the West. The Louisiana Purchase, regardless of what you think of its legality, did not include parts of the Spanish empire in the southwest. When Mexico became independent it took control of these areas, although it did very little to develop them. Missionaries were sent North, first from Spanish Mexico and then from independent Mexico, but there were few settlers. A church or mission with a small garrison was the typical Mexican operation and there were not many of them.[18]

American settlers, however, moved across the Mississippi. Most of the early ones were from the south and brought their slaves and when they were admitted as states, they enacted slave codes. Once again, it should be kept in mind that the first Presidents except for Adams were slaveholders. The French Republic had freed all the slaves in its territory. It is not obvious whether Napoleon intended to keep this law, and

---

[18] One of the most beautiful is a church near Tucson. I recommend my readers visit it. The building is obviously Spanish but the murals on the interior show strong Indian influence.

more particularly, whether it would have banned slavery in the newly acquired Louisiana territory.

When thinking of "what might have been" you can easily imagine that if Adams had remained President he might have made slavery illegal in the newly acquired territories. Certainly Jefferson a large scale slave owner, also deeply in debt, would not.

If the newly admitted areas west of the Mississippi had come in as non-slave states, with the corresponding reduction of Senators and Electors from slave holding states, the Civil war might have been avoided. As I have mentioned several time previously, speculation on a different course of history is amusing, but only speculation.

Texas however was part of Mexico and at first was organized as a Mexican province. Slavery was illegal in Mexico, but that did not seem to have impeded it in Texas when the southern settlers brought their slaves with them. Indeed there was a considerable trade in shipping slaves to Texas. Eventually, however, the Texans revolted and won their war of independence.[19]

To repeat the discussion above, the Texans did not really want independence; they wanted to enter the United States. At first, however, they had difficulty. The war had upset some Americans and the fact that they would be a slave state may have made a difference. Slavery was beginning to become a significant political issue in the United States.

---

[19] The Battle of the San Jacinto was militarily interesting. The Texan army carried out a surprise attack on the center of the Mexican force, across open fields, and in broad daylight. The Mexicans were on siesta.

When admitted Texas claimed a border with Mexico which was farther south than the Mexicans admitted. There was a clash between the US and the Mexican troops in the disputed area and President Polk was able to convince Congress that they should declare war.[20] It seems clear that Polk wanted war and deliberately provoked the Mexicans. There was, however, a serious problem. He had announced that he was not the candidate for another term, but nevertheless objected to a successful general running for president. Thus he was less than fully supportive of the U.S. military effort.

The war started in northern Mexico but, after a United States victory at Buena Vista, Scott, then commander of the American army, took an amphibious expedition to Vera Cruz and followed in the track of Cortez to Mexico City.

President Polk sent down a diplomat to negotiate a treaty of peace. The man he chose was the chief clerk of the Department of State who spoke fluent Spanish. He was also as it turned out an admirer of Spanish culture and drew the border more or less where it is now rather than further south. This was in accordance with his instructions, but I wish he had violated them a little bit thus putting the border further south. The real estate south of the border was not very valuable, but it would have shortened the border and hence made

---

[20] Lincoln, who at that time was in the House of Representatives, made an unsuccessful effort to convince his colleagues that the action was in the disputed territories.

policing it easier. Incidentally, his credentials were withdrawn before he signed the treaty. The Senate ratified it anyway.[21]

Polk was annoyed by the treaty and for, a while talked about putting the diplomat in jail. The treaty was with Mexico but not with the Indians and the Americans had to suppress them too. Geronimo was one of the United States most difficult opponents in this "pacification" operation and his territory was mainly north of the new border. The Americans also shortly, thereafter, purchased another small piece of real estate, the Gadsden Purchase, in order to get possession of a pass through the Rockies. Here again they bought from the Mexicans and not from the Indians.

If anything the Indians in the new area were harder to deal with than those in the eastern part of the United States. But by this time the railroad had been developed. The Americans built railroads for commercial reasons, but they could be used to move troops. There was also the telegraph. Altogether, driving the Indians into reservations in the late 19th-century was fairly easily accomplished although it took some time and blood.

If California was exempted, the area obtained directly west of Texas was mainly desert or semi-desert. In the early days there were few farmers there, but cattle raising was possible. There were also various minerals which could be dug up. California, for example, had gold. It was, of course, inhabited by Indians but they were few

---

[21] See discussion of Gadsden Purchase below.

and weak. They were dealt with in the same way as the eastern Indians.

The U.S. border with Canada raised a number of minor difficulties over time. In the first place, the diplomats in Paris negotiating the end of the Revolutionary war used a defective map to draw the northern boundary of Maine. The land concerned was not a very large area, but it was good farming land. A peaceful compromise was drawn up and has stuck ever since. I mentioned above that the British apparently thought that Canada was not defensible against an American attack after they had settled the area west of the Appalachians.

There were number of other cases in which the Canadian boundary was not clear. Some of them were quite sizable. The English had good claims in pure law to most of Washington and Oregon. The Willamette Valley, however, was excellent farmland and attracted covered wagon trains from the East. Thus there was a significant population of American farmers. Since English had only a few trading posts they gave up the two states to the United States. There was then a considerable doubt as to exactly where the western end of the boundary went. Once again there was a fairly peaceful settlement. It should be said that the United States normally was willing to submit these difficulties to arbitration, and granted the military weakness in the area of England they also favored arbitration.

The United States had peacefully purchased Alaska from Russia, perhaps overpaying for it. The border of the Panhandle of Alaska with Canada was uncertain. President Grant actually sent some troops there to pin down the American claims. In view of the general worthlessness of the land, however, once again, a peaceful arrangement could be made.

Hawaii was more complicated. It had been independent kingdom ruled by a dynasty of natives. A number of Americans moved in with the purpose of raising sugar and then with the aid of a cruiser, which happened to be in port, overthrew the dynasty, intending to be annexed by the United States. The Congress was unhappy about all of this and refused to annex them for a while, and eventually made them a territory instead of a state. It was not until the 1950s that they eventually became a state at the same time as Alaska.

Midway, which on the map looks like a very distant extension of the Hawaiian island chain, was unoccupied and a visiting American ship claimed it well before the United States acquired Hawaii. Wake, even farther out was acquired largely as part of Pan American Airways desired to build a transpacific air route. The distance that their big flying boats could cover between the refueling stops was short enough so that it was necessary to put refueling facilities on Wake. They added a small resort hotel. It was also given a small garrison of Marines just before the outbreak of the war. The Japanese took it easily. One of the reasons for the Japanese success at Pearl Harbor was the fact that the three aircraft carriers, which were all that were left in the Pacific Fleet after Roosevelt's transfer of a sizeable part of the Pacific fleet to the Atlantic, had gone off to Wake for the purpose of delivering its air garrison.

I have covered most of the things that the United States engaged in as far as foreign policy was concerned, between the end of the war of 1812 and their contratemps with Spain. However, there were a large number of minor problems. Before the Civil War, the United States had a large merchant Marine and a very active foreign trade. This led to a large number of minor difficulties with various countries. I had some personal experience with this kind of thing. My first Foreign Service job was as Vice-Counsel in the Consulate-General in Tientsin. This involved the same kind of thing that made up so much of the work of the diplomatic service in the 19th-century. In addition to worrying about the American citizens in the north China area and doing various minor administrative tasks, I was involved in some difficulties between the American business and the locals.

To give the most important example (which shows how unimportant most of them were) during the short period in which the Marines were in occupation of Tientsin, a few of them were in temporary occupation of a British owned warehouse full of cotton. It caught fire shortly after the Marines left. The British thought it was the Marines' carelessness and the Marines thought that they were above all criticism. I investigated and decided that it probably was the result of the Marines' carelessness. As a recent graduate from a law school, I wrote a long memorandum on the subject which was convincing enough so that the Americans paid for the damages.

This kind of thing was the bulk of the work of the Americans widespread diplomatic service in much of the 19th-century. Bemis devotes much space to the matter. Since he has done such a good job, and frankly, because the subject bores me, I decided to skip this long collection of minor diplomatic controversies. Due to the activities of the Southern Raiders, the U.S. merchant marine was less impressive after the Civil War. They still however were a major participant in world trade. This again led to a number of minor difficulties which were solved diplomatically. They fairly frequently accepted arbitration. If the reader is curious on this matter, I suggest that he turn to Bemis.

Chapter 9

European Empires

I have now finished with the diplomatic history of the United States as what I shall call a colonial country. In the latter decade of the 19th-century and through out the 20th-century (hopefully also the 21st-century) the U.S. foreign policy was mainly directed outside of its continental mainland. Before turning to this latter part of the foreign policy, I would like to digress to consider other countries which by 1900 had seized a great deal of real estate and hence had large geographic scope.

There had been a great deal of grabbing of land in Europe, but because of the balance of power, it was still broken up into small countries. Many of these small countries had, however, acquired quite extensive real estate holdings in other parts of world. They were like the United States in that they held quite extensive territories, but unlike the Americans they had not driven out the natives. These areas were still held by their original inhabitants with, in most cases, only a few European colonists, soldiers and governors. Let me turn to these now.

More on Portugal

While exploring the route to India, the Portuguese navigators had got a good idea of the prevailing winds in the south Atlantic. They realized that their sail powered ships had to go well west of the bulge of Africa in order to get south. As a result, one of their ships accidentally discovered Brazil some years after Columbus. Further exploration revealed the long coast and the fact that the area along the coast was a set of fairly low mountains and hills thinly occupied by very backward Indians.

Rather quickly they realized that the area could be used to raise sugar, and for this purpose they imported slaves from Africa. The hump of Brazil is closer to Africa than almost any other part of the American continents. Further, they already had some trading posts along the African coast. Thus purchasing slaves from the native chiefs was easy. They probably did not have as heavy a death toll on the relatively short trip across the Atlantic as ships carrying slaves to northern parts of the American continent did.[22]

Brazil thus developed a significant sugar export, but in time the development of the Caribbean islands by European powers, also using slave labor imported from Africa, cut into their market seriously. It should be said that the death rate on the island plantations was

---

[22] The death rate on the middle passage was high, but the death rate on ships carrying Irish immigrants to the northern colonies was also high. Since these immigrants were mainly indentured, the ship owner's profit in both areas depended on how many live bodies were delivered at the end.

extremely high, and that included both the white overseers and the slaves. At one time it was thought that these islands were the most important and wealthy of European colonies because of their sugar production.

It is to me something of mystery that the Europeans in the east, for a long period, made no effort to extend their holdings outside their trading posts. It wasn't till Clive's great victory at Plassey which gave the honorable East India Company one province in India, that the colonial powers held any significant amount of real estate outside their trading posts in the east. There were two minor exceptions; the Dutch put some farmers ashore in the Cape of Good Hope in order to provide fresh fruit and vegetables to their ships on the way to Indonesia. They also seized a couple of small islands where the spices were grown. The Portugese made small settlements in Mozambique and Angola.

All of this was very minor compared to the large empires created in the 19th-century. The 19th-century empires were all created by democracies. England, the Dutch, Belgium, France, and, as a late-comer, Imperial Germany all seized areas many times as large as the metropolitan countries. It's hard to argue that these were exploitative, since the colonial powers, with the possible exception of Belgium, gave governments better than those which they replaced and, in many cases, better than what eventually replaced the colonial governments.

It should be repeated that the early English economists normally thought that the empire cost more than the benefit. This is particularly surprising since John Stuart Mill was a son of an official of the Honorable East India Company. There are few modern studies of the matter, but I think that the view of those economists is generally accepted today.

The officials and soldiers who won their reputations and good salaries normally favored the empires and took steps to expand them. During most of the period of the 19th-century, however, the death rate for white officials sent out to places like India was very high. When Arthur Wellesley went out to India to join his brother, he had only a 50% chance of coming back alive. There were similar statistics for the other colonies until the later part of the century when medicine began to get a hold on such diseases as malaria and yellow fever. Thus the people who went out to the Imperial possessions had even shorter life expectancies than the people who stayed home.

Since 1890, The Modern Period

Between 1815 and 1890, the U.S. foreign policy fell in two general segments, the seizure and settlement of the West, and general, but not complete, indifference to anything east of their initial states. With the completion of their conquest and settlement of the West the major, and very successful, aspect of their foreign policy was completed. There were various other empty areas in the world which the United States could have annexed with profit, but made no effort to do so. They could also have followed the European powers in seizing territory already occupied for the purpose of ruling the previous inhabitants. Once again, they did not do so.

What did the Americans do after the completion of the conquest of the United States? They undertook wars which were largely moral in purpose. They failed to establish a highly moral world, but they did attack several countries which the Americans regarded as representing wickedness. Let me begin with their war with Spain. If I understand the standard history of this event, it was set off by a revolt against Spain in Cuba. The Spaniards were putting the revolt down using fairly cruel methods. There happened to be a circulation war going on in New York City newspapers and they gave a great deal of prominence to the Spanish cruelty. At this point, the American battleship Maine which was in the Harbor of Havana was sunk by an explosion.

To this day, it is not completely clear what caused the explosion. It might have been an accidental magazine explosion. Such things were not unknown among navies of the time. The wreckage, however, seemed to point to an external explosion. The United States, in any event, took the view that the Spanish government had done it and after a delay declared war.[23]

At the time the war did not look so simple and easy as it does retrospectively. Many European observers, for example, thought that the Spanish navy was superior to the Americans. This was disproved in Manila Bay and off Santiago. The U.S. army, largely hastily mobilized volunteers, won quickly in Cuba. In the Philippines, they had more trouble. The Spaniards promptly surrendered Manila, but the Filipinos who wanted independence organized a guerilla war against the American forces.[24] This lasted quite a while and developed into a minor but nasty war in which they "Civilized them with a Krag". Eventually they set up a democratic local government with, after

---

[23] My father, who spoke fluent Spanish and was in Cuba somewhat later selling agricultural machinery, was convinced that the mine had been set off by the rebels in hopes that the Americans would blame Spain.

[24] Little Brown Brother, Leon Wolf, History Book Club, New York, 1960 covers the guerilla war in detail. Interestingly, the author is very anti-American.

a short delay, a former guerrilla commander as President. They were to receive full independence in 1943. Since at that time they were under the Japanese occupation, their independence was delayed.

The Muslims who had fought a long guerilla war against Spain in the southern part of the Philippines kept it up when the United States took over. Anticipating recent developments in Iraq, individuals called "juramentados" engaged in suicide attacks on the American troops. Since they used knives instead of bombs, the casualties were low. It was found that the 38 pistol carried by officers was inadequate to stop them, so the 45 became the standard officers' weapon. The guerrilla movement was not totally repressed, and indeed, is still going on in the southern islands of the Philippines.

Cuba also was set up as an independent country with a democratic government. The treaty granting independence provided that the Americans could come back if they ceased to be a democracy. As part of Roosevelt's good neighbor policy, this provision in the treaty was eliminated. This was intended as a gesture of goodwill, but Cuba since that time has suffered under a number of unpleasant dictatorships. Castro damaged their economy so severely that prostitution is one of their main foreign currency sources.

Neither in Cuba nor in the Philippines can the United States claim to have made direct gains of any sort. They can say that they entered the war to "do good" and in fact could perhaps claim that they did leave the world somewhat better than it was before. This is by no means certain, however. To repeat, after World War II almost all of the colonies obtained independence either through small wars or as a free gift. The few remaining Spanish colonies after the United States had removed Cuba, and the Philippines were given their independence. It seems likely that Cuba and the Philippines would have received their independence also if the Americans had not fought the Spanish war.

This leaves Guam and Puerto Rico still under the U.S. control. Guam is pretty, but of no significant value. Puerto Rico could have either independence or admission to the United States as a state, but their financial situation with respect to the government in Washington is very superior. Occasionally there are demands for either independence or statehood, but they seem happy with their present status.

With respect to the northern part of the Philippines, the Americans could have converted them into a standard European-type colony with a population subject to control from the homeland. Since the Filipinos were Catholic, however, and mainly could speak Spanish, this would be somewhat out of the ordinary run of American expansion. As another possibility, they could have made the Philippines one or more states. So far as I know the project was never even seriously contemplated. The Americans did institute a major effort to teach them English.

The southern Philippines had never been successfully pacified by the Spaniards and, as mentioned above, were largely occupied by Mohammedans. The area wasn't very densely settled, however, and I suppose that, theoretically, the Americans could have introduced agricultural settlers. In any event, it remained a military problem for the United States and for the Filipinos when they took over. It still is.

The United States may speculate on what would have happened had they not got into the war. I presume that the Spaniards would have been able to put down the rebellion in Cuba as they previously had done with the Philippines. Whether they would have produced a poorer government than these places actually received is an object of speculation. But, to bore the reader with further repetition, all of the other colonial powers gave up their colonies after World War II. It seems likely that Spain also would have done so if they had retained their empire. They did in fact give up their few African holdings.

But this is speculation and no more. It is clear that the statement that Cuba and the Philippines gained is also speculation, but in the opposite direction.

In a way this war will serve as a model for the American wars in the 20th-century. As a general rule, they got into them for no very clear cut material motives, and made little in the way of material gain. Moral principles, in particular the desire to penalize aggression by anyone, except themselves dealing with the Indians, seem to have been their major motives.

In both World War I and World War II, it is possible to argue that in the long run the United States would have had trouble if countries which had been beaten by their intervention had won and turned against them, which they might have. The Americans should remember that Japan an ally in World War I was an enemy in World War II.

Further after the United States had saved Russia in World War II, the Americans were on the verge of war with her for a long time. Historic speculation is fun, but it is speculation and no more.

If ignoring vulgar calculations of profit and loss and turning to moral and emotional motives, then World War I and World War II were great successes. In both cases, the enemies ended prostrated and a very strong feeling that the Americans had achieved a great victory. In both cases, they seemed to have felt that it was the final war and they would from then on have peace. In both cases, an organization was set up which was intended to guarantee *that* peace and, although the Americans refused to actually go into the League of Nations, its establishment was very largely an American accomplishment. The veto in the United Nations[25] protects the United States from any policies it might have which would inconvenience them. Although the Americans have pushed for the establishment of various international courts, they normally refuse to give them jurisdiction over their citizens. The current effort to establish an international criminal court without jurisdiction over Americans is typical. The end product in both wars was disappointing although, so far, not as disappointing after World War II as after World War I.

At the moment the United States is in great, but not widely perceived, danger. There are at least 10 countries with nuclear weapons and smuggling them across borders into major cities seems not at all

---

[25] If the charter of the League were ratified, the United States would also have had veto power.

impossible. Delivering nucleur weapons by rockets also seems well within the bounds of possibility even for a minor power. Starting a deadly epidemic is also possible and might kill many, many people. So far as I know there is no country which would dare to do either to them. Only a few nuclear weapons states could destroy them in one blow, and hence be safe. Let's hope that this continues to be the case. Still the situation is dangerous and it is a readily predictable outcome of their policy.

Indeed in the years right after World War II a great many politically motivated scientists did predict that something like this would occur. So far it is merely a hazard, and a hazard that has remained only potential. Let's hope it continues in that state, but I wish the Americans could depend on something stronger than hope.

Chapter 11

Between the Wars (Part 1)

So far my history has roughly paralleled that of Bemis.[26] The parallel is, however, only rough. He hardly mentions the American conquest of the continent from the Indians. I suspected he feels this was not part of the diplomatic history, since it was very undiplomatic. When he does briefly mention the Indians it is usually in connection with the U.S. relations with some foreign power. It should I think be said; that his book mainly deals with trivia before 1890. The United States had minor dealings with many countries, and these Bemis chronicles in great detail. So far as I know no one has ever raised any questions about his documentation. Certainly I found him an excellent guide to what, in my opinion, are unimportant matters.

In a way his book illustrates both the strength and weakness of American academic research. Obviously a great deal of work was done and so far as I know no one has criticized his research even for minor details. On the other hand, other than rising in the scholarly community, it's hard to see why he put in so much work. To repeat, in a way

---

[26] Diplomatic History of the United States, Henry Flagg Bemis, New York, Henry Holt, And Company, 1952.

it is an example of both the strength and weakness of modern scholarly activity in universities. He no doubt was able to use his book in the usual wars within faculties for prestige and what little power scholarly success might give. Further, I suppose reading the book would have been helpful for people intending to enter the diplomatic service in the 19th-century. The world has changed however, and I doubt that it would be of much help now.[27]

To some extent he deals with the expansion of the United States. The Mexican war was thoroughly dealt with as was the Gadsden Purchase. In addition, the United States had a number of problems with other countries, they bought the Louisiana Purchase, for example, and Andrew Jackson invaded Florida with the result that they acquired that state without very much consideration of moral principles.

The part of the work of Bemis which he covers extensively and which is relative to the U.S. geographic expansion, concerns a number of minor difficulties with England mainly concerning the Canadian border. To repeat, the maps used in the negotiations in Paris at the end of the Revolutionary war were inaccurate. As a result, the northern boundary of Maine had to be redrawn. The English were generous and the Americans acquired some valuable farmland. The western boundary was even more sorely undetermined and here again the United States had to undertake negotiations with England. The end

---

[27] I had not read the book or his numerous articles before or during my short career as a diplomat.

product was more or less what they now have, and the negotiations never showed any real signs of war.[28]

When the United States purchased Alaska the border between the Russia possessions and Canada was not firmly demarcated. At one point President Grant sent some troops to their claimed border as a gesture, but a peaceful outcome resulted. The western part of the line beyond Vancouver, was also peacefully negotiated by way of an arbitration treaty.

Other than this, the monumental scholarship of Bemis deals with essentially minor matters. The United States, except their wars with England, Mexico, and Spain, there were enough differences with other countries for Bemis to fill a thick volume, but mostly they were unimportant.

The scholarship exhibited by Bemis in much of his lengthy book is, in my opinion, rather wasted because of the minor nature of the problems. In a way, it is an example of the kind of scholarly research which fills the time of distinguished Professors but doesn't really make the world any better off. I congratulate him on his industry and skill, but wish it had been applied elsewhere. His writing style is excellent and I positively enjoyed reading the book. Unfortunately, I think that people not specifically interested in his field would find it a waste of time except perhaps for entertainment.

---

[28] The slogan 'Fifty–Four Forty or Fight' was a popular cry, but apparently it was not seriously pushed."

As a general rule, Bemis approves of the U.S. foreign policy up to the outbreak of the war with Spain. From then on, including the settlement of that war, he usually disapproves. Since this is in accord with my own feelings, I do not say this in a spirit of criticism. He disapproves of the Spanish war and its outcome, and also of the outcome of World War I in so far as that outcome involved an effort to establish permanent peace. Bemis does not think that that this is a likely outcome. History since he completed his book confirms his pessimism. The book ran through many revisions. The one I have is the 1952 edition.

World War II changed the international situation, and in particular the role of the United States. They are now deeply involved in almost everything that happens in the world as far as foreign policy is concerned. It's hard to argue that they have done a particularly good job in this area. World War II has been followed by a number of wars which they think of as minor but which caused a good deal of bloodshed. Interestingly the biggest of these wars, the establishment of the Communist government in China, is rarely mentioned in American foreign policy discussion, although their arms embargo on the Nationalists played a major role in the outcome.

Chapter 12
World War I

A great deal has been written about the origins of World War I, and I do not intend to add to it. Essentially Europe was divided into two camps and the assassination of the heir to the Austro-Hungarian throne set off the war. The only surprise was that Italy, allied with Germany and Austria–Hungary, was late in her entry into the war and then came in on the side of France and England against her formal allies.

It has only recently been revealed that England had a secret agreement with France under which they would enter a war between France and Germany on France's side. Balance of power considerations would, of course, have pointed towards preventing German dominance of Europe. When the war broke out, nominally England entered the war because of the invasion of Belgium by the Germans. They would have come in anyway.

Almost 100 years before, Belgium had been created and a general treaty guaranteeing their neutrality was signed. The Belgians obviously did not put much confidence in that treaty because they heavily fortified their frontier and built an excellent small army. The German army swinging north of the heavy French fortifications on their frontier went into Belgium and came very close to winning at the very beginning of the war. They failed at the Marne, however, and the invasion of Germany by Russia, allied with France, meant that they had to put many of their troops in the east and hence could not spare enough forces for prompt victory in the west.

England, of course, entered and put Germany under blockade. It should be said that this blockade violated international law on the subject. During the American Civil War, the British insisted that the blockade had to be a "close" blockade. They ruled that unless the ships outside the port were so close as to endanger a ship attempting to enter the blockaded port, the blockade was illegal. This caused the U.S. Navy blockading the south some trouble.

It is arguable, although not by any means certain, that the German navy was built to prevent this kind of blockade of Germany. It certainly would have been impossible in 1914 and in fact the English made no effort to impose this kind of blockade which they had earlier occasionally maintained was the only legal type. Instead, they simply intercepted ships either in English Channel or the northern part of the North Sea. This led to some, but not very serious, diplomatic difficulties with the United States.

There is no point in going through the details of the land fighting. They are the subject, once again, of many books. In terms of casualties and destruction, it was one of the worst wars ever fought. The Americans got in late and their casualties were comparatively light. The history of their military operations will be dealt with below.

From the beginning there was a propaganda war directed at the United States. The English had dredged up the German cables so direct communication with the United States was difficult for the Germans. Radio was still rather primitive in those days. In addition, in my opinion, the English were just much better propagandists than the Germans. Further the British and French war orders kept the Americans financial system and some of their manufacturing facilities prosperous.

England having placed their blockade on Germany, the Germans responded by introducing submarine warfare. The German submarines sank ships attempting to reach France and England, and since there were Americans traveling on these ships, some Americans were killed. The Americans denounced this operation and after the sinking of the Lusitania, the Germans temporarily stopped it. Wilson made a number of severe statements threatening Germany about the submarines which he thought were immoral, and when the Germans renewed their submarine blockade, he asked the Congress to declare war, which it did.

It is ironic that in World War II, the Americans promptly announced unrestricted submarine warfare against the Japanese a few days after Pearl Harbor. So far as I know, no neutral country objected to this use of submarines. Certainly, none of them declared war because of it.

The situation in the east when the United States entered World War I was surprisingly similar to the present situation. Russia was in the state of collapse and shortly would temporarily breakup. The Baltic countries had been set up by the Germans as constitutional monarchies with German princelings as their kings. The Ukraine was independent with the prospect that it would have a member of the Austro-Hungarian House of Hapsburg as its constitutional monarch. Russia itself was, temporarily, a democracy.

The parts of the former Russian empire occupied by people of Turkish origin and speaking languages in the Turkish family were in a state of confusion. The British had even sent a small expeditionary force across the Himalayas. War prisoners from the Austro-Hungarian forces had organized a Royal and Imperial East Battalion there. The Caucasus was independent and broken up into a set of small countries with generally Republican governments, rather similar to the present situation. Parts of it were under the Turkish occupation.

Germany was able to withdraw troops from the eastern front and undertook a major offensive in France. The offensive was only moderately successful. It seems likely that if the Americans had not entered, a peace would have been patched up between the western allies and Germany. Germany did not show any signs of wanting to annex any part of France, although perhaps they would have split Belgium along ethnic lines. They might have forced French disarmament on the same lines as the Allied disarmament of Germany at Versailles.[29]

---

[29] I occasionally receive propaganda from the Flemish independence movement. I only glance at it, but it is clear that it is still alive.

Probably Germany would have increased the size of her African empire. Austria–Hungary and Bulgaria were in occupation of most of the Balkans, but the prospect that Austria–Hungary would breakup was real. Serbia would not have been expanded into Yugoslavia. The present disintegration of Yugoslavia is some indication that the unification was unpopular among the minor ethnic groups there.[30]

Turkey, when the United States declared war, still held much of modern Iraq, and their forces in Palestine were fairly far south. In both cases they were simply holding parts of the prewar Turkish Empire. The British had pushed north in what is now Iraq and Palestine. The remaining Turkish position in both of these places was basically a not completely successful defense of their prewar property.

To engage in a little speculation of what might have been, I have always thought that the dissolution of the Austro-Hungarian Empire was a major tragedy. The expansion of Serbia into Yugoslavia has recently been demonstrated to be a mistake in the long-run. The basic problem was that nationalism was a fad at the time. Giving every small group of people their own nation was something that Woodrow Wilson and many other people thought was morally compulsory. It was not, of course, applied when it would advantage the Americans' former enemies.

The division of the Austro-Hungarian Empire, although in general along national lines, was by no means exact. Some Hungarians found

---

[30] The American very small scale intervention in the disturbances in former Yugoslavia led to anti-American riots against the American Embassy in Peking. I doubt that anyone in 1918 would have even imagined such an outcome from the splitting of the Austro-Hungarian Empire.

themselves living in Romania, and Czechoslovakia was given borders that included many Germans. Altogether, the tinder for future wars was scattered over Eastern Europe.

If the Americans had not entered, it seems likely that Germany would have tried again in France and then there would have been a patched up peace. To repeat what I said above, the German politicians did not particularly want to include a number of French citizens as voters in the German Reich. My guess would be that Germany would have acquired a good deal more of Africa and those parts of former Turkey which were at the moment under British occupation would have been given back. Turkey might have acquired areas in the Caucasus and a portion of that part of central Asia occupied by people speaking Turkish languages.

The German army would probably have insisted on some kind of democracy in Russia, the independent Ukraine, the Baltic states, and possibly some of the Turkish tribes in Central Asia. Thus the area would have reached in 1918 more or less what it in fact reached in the 1990s.

Whether the situation would have remained stable is obviously an open question. It's by no means clear, however, that the present situation in that area is stable. In the war, a good deal of blood was shed imposing a temporary (80 year) reorganization of the area. It may be, of course, that the present situation is also only temporary.

But let me leave this speculation on what might have been and deal with what actually did happen. To repeat what I said above,

British and French propaganda was vastly better than the German's. The alleged German atrocities in Belgium were presented with great skill and vigor.

Another point which is normally ignored here is hyper-Americanism. Americans are, of course, all descendents from immigrants. The only difference is how long ago their ancestors crossed the Atlantic. If it was fairly recent, then hyper-Americanism can be a problem. A certain amount of displaced patriotism for their ancestors' native land is not surprising. As it happens, many more of us, including the author, descend from English stock than from any other. Thus a certain amount of pro-English sentiment should be expected in talking about the U.S. foreign affairs.

In the particular case of World War I this was more than usually important, because Wilson's mother was English. Further his principal foreign policy adviser, Col. House, had both an English mother and an English father. I know of no careful study of the possible effect of this ancestry on their foreign policy. I hope I will stimulate one of my readers to engage in such a study. I should perhaps, parenthetically, point out that Acheson's father was Anglican bishop of Connecticut and his mother was also English. In their household the King's health was toasted every year on his birthday. Once again I would like some research on whether this had any affect on the American policy in World War II, and its aftermath.

But to return to the war, the United States had built up an excellent Navy in the early 20th-century, but it was more or less irrelevant to the war. England and, for that matter if we count its allies France and Italy, had much more naval power than Germany and its ally Austria–Hungary. The U.S. destroyers were helpful in protecting convoys against submarines, but the bulk of the surface fleet spent the war in harbor.

The Americans had very little in the way of an army or an Air Force. Even in equipment, although they had been supplying the allies with much material, they were drastically short and had to borrow from the allies much of their equipment. As a striking example Rickenbacker became America's first ace flying a French plane. They were better off with equipment for the army on the ground, but still short of many things.

In personnel the Americans were particularly short since they had only a very few people in the army. Shortly before they entered the war, a Mexican bandit named Villa had raided an American city, killing about 40 American citizens. General Pershing was sent with what they had in the way of an army into Mexico to catch him. There was also a minor marine operation at Vera Cruz. It turned out, however, that Villa could run faster than Pershing could advance. After a while Wilson grew tired of the operation and withdrew Pershing. All this was distressing, particularly since Wilson had always been publicly against intervening in Latin America and his Secretary of the State, Bryan was a pacifist. Failing in his one intervention must have been a severe disappointment. In spite of his failure in Mexico, when they entered the war Pershing was appointed commander of the U.S. forces in France.

If the United States has stayed out and a peace was patched up, it's hard to argue that the world would have been worse off than in the actual peace settlement. Speculation on historical developments is both fun and intellectually valuable. To do a little of such speculation, Lenin and Stalin would have remained minor political figures on the left. Hitler would have been a second-rate painter. Russia in any event would have escaped the deadly reign of Lenin and Stalin, and the western European Jewish population would have survived. Would the Americans have had World War II? My crystal ball gets hazy after such a long period.

Retrospectively, it's a little hard to argue that the Americans' entry into the war was wise or that it had good results. I have conducted a very small opinion poll among younger people who are currently engaged in lobbying in Washington. Only one out of eleven knew that the Americans entered because of submarine warfare. And to repeat, they carried out exactly the kind of submarine warfare to which they objected in 1917 in the Pacific in World War II.

To return to World War I, the Americans had only a small professional army although some efforts had been made to prepare it for a major war. This professional army had to be broken up in order to provide instructors for the newly drafted forces. The movement of this very large army across the Atlantic to France changed the balance of power in the war in Europe very sharply. Not only did the allies now have many more troops, but the American forces were fresh and not worn down by a long period of combat. As a patriotic American,

I can be proud of the fighting capacity of these troops. The Americans drove the Germans back and would no doubt have forced the Rhine and pushed the battles actually into Germany had not the German system collapsed.

The fall of Germany, although mainly the result of the introduction of large numbers of American troops, had more effect in Eastern Europe than in the west. The Franco-German border was moved back to more or less where it had been before 1870, but the changes in Eastern Europe were much more drastic. Austria–Hungary collapsed and the small states which Germany had created along the Baltic were retained as independent countries. Serbia annexed parts of the collapsed Austro-Hungarian Empire. Recent developments in the area indicate that this was a mistake. Poland not only became independent, but became very large and included unhappy minorities. Altogether it was not a very stable situation.

Russia was temporarily broken up. The Germans had moved Lenin from Switzerland to Russia, and provided him with substantial financial resources. He took advantage of this to overthrow the temporary democracy which had been established in the Russian part of the former Russian empire. As mentioned above, the situation in Russia was much like it is now with the Ukraine temporarily independent, the Turkish states in Central Asia in a state of confusion, and the small states in the Caucasus independent.

There was then a Civil War between the Whites and the Reds with the Whites attempting to reestablish the ancient regime. England and the United States both made minor efforts to assist the Whites. The United States, for example, had a small expeditionary Force near Vladivostok for some time. In the war itself, however, the Reds won. There were two basic reasons other than simply good command. In the first place, the Reds had decided to break up the noble estates and this gave them the support of many peasants. In the second place, however, they had much more ammunition. The bulk of the ammunition supplies accumulated by the czarist armies were stored in the area held by the Reds. In consequence, they had much more ammunition than the Whites.

The war, however, went on for quite a while, the Ukraine was suppressed fairly quickly but the small republics in the Caucasus held out for several years. In the Turkish areas in Central Asia, a guerilla war continued almost throughout the 1920s. As a sort of byproduct of the collapse of the Chinese empire, the new communist state was able to reestablish essential control over inner Mongolia and northern Manchuria. Outer Mongolia became a Russian puppet state. So the new Russian empire was a little bigger in Asia than had been the old empire.

Western Germany was occupied by Allied troops, interestingly, MacArthur was one of the commanders. Not only was the border of Germany pushed back to the line drawn by Louis the XIV, but the Saar was detached. Getting it back was one of the first of Hitler's accomplishments.

The United States withdrew their forces from Europe very early and in fact demobilized them so that once again they had only a very small army. The U.S. navy remained large, indeed after the naval disarmament conference we shared with England the honor of having the largest forces at sea. Japan, of course, had a big navy, and the naval forces of France and Italy were by no means contemptible.

England demobilized the conscript forces that she had depended on for ground forces in World War I into a rather small professional army. As soon as the war broke out again, they were able to expand it reasonably fast. Most of the rest of the continental powers retained conscription and had quite large armies. Until Hitler tore up the Treaty of Versailles, the German army was restricted, but it rapidly grew in the 1930s. His ally, Italy had a large but incompetent army.

Chapter 13
Between the Wars (Part 2)

It may seem out of place but it seems to me that I should begin my discussion of the interwar period by dealing with the peace negotiations for World War I. In a way the war ended with the armistice agreement, and the negotiations in Paris for a final settlement took place in a period when no fighting was undertaken. Parts of Western Germany in fact were occupied, and the German army and navy were reduced to impotence. Austria–Hungary had fallen apart, and although there was still some fighting and an existing army in Turkey, to say that the war was over is reasonable, and so I will begin my discussion of the interwar period with the signature of the armistice.

Woodrow Wilson wanted to establish an international government which would prevent future wars. This was on the whole in accord with the preferences of the other allies, although in most cases they had other objectives too.

France in particular wanted to collect gigantic reparations from Germany and make certain the Germans remained disarmed. They went along with Wilson's ideas, and indeed a French Premiere presided over the meeting to establish the peace and the new organization which was intended to make peace permanent. It is to me dubious that any of the people that led the other allies really were sincere in their public statements. There was no reason to quarrel with the United States and it was a perfect possible that the arrangement would mean that the United States would be militarily involved in any future war in Europe.

Wilson had not made sure that he would have American support for his ideas and indeed the eventual outcome was that the Senate refused to ratify the Versailles Treaty. The United States had to enter into separate peace agreements with Germany and its allies. Wilson's joint negotiations with the allies and with the Senate have been heavily criticized. Of course he was ill during the latter period of the negotiations, so I suppose he cannot be really criticized. In any event, the Senate refused to ratify and the United States did not become a member of the League of Nations.

Indeed the generally Republican Senate and President after the election were strongly opposed to the League. I cannot guess why they thought it was positively harmful when in fact it was pretty much harmless, but they did seem to take that attitude. For example, the American Consul in Geneva was ordered to never set foot in the building of the League. In almost every other way, the American government refused to cooperate with the League.

This has been heavily criticized, but, in my opinion, did little harm. The League's equivalent of the Security Council and its successor required unanimous consent to any serious activity. Almost all the countries that might have undertaken aggressive wars were members of the Council and hence the League could do nothing against them. The League took no serious efforts against the immediately out breaking minor wars. The Russian invasion of Poland was stopped but by Polish forces without anything more than some language by the League. Japan which was rather slowly beginning the conquest of China by improving their position in Manchuria was completely unimpeded by the League in the 1920s. Japan, of course, had veto power in the equivalent of the Security Council; but, more on this later.

The United States, as a result of their successful participation in World War I, was now generally recognized as a great power and tended to get involved in various international affairs. On the whole, however, they played a less prominent role in these matters than their size and power would have indicated.

I have so far largely ignored the U.S. relations with the southern part of the Americas. In general these were minor, with small American military units getting involved in small countries. They had forced the independence of Panama in order to build the canal and Roosevelt thought that since they were pressuring other powers to refrain from using force in the Americas countries, they had a duty to put pressure on South American countries to do things like paying their debts. This was called the Roosevelt Corollary to the Monroe Doctrine. This irritated their Latin neighbors a great deal, but normally involved only very minor military activities by the Marines.

The island that used to be called Hispanola while still part of European colonial empires, was divided in two parts with Haiti speaking French and the Dominican Republic speaking Spanish. For a while they were governed by American military forces with one half under the army and one half under the marines. The Americans were not popular but an examination of the Hispanola history after they left seems to indicate that they benefited them a good deal. Granted the present situation in Haiti, I should think there would be at least some nostalgia for the former occupation.

In general, South American intellectuals resented the U.S. activities and were happy when the Americans adopted the good neighbor policy. Hoover, of course, was a Quaker and hence did not like the idea of having troops under his command in active combat south of their borders. He began a withdrawal of the troops and introduced the "good neighbor" policy. This policy is normally mainly connected with Roosevelt, but Hoover actually started it although Roosevelt did much more to implement it.

In the 1920s, probably the most important single thing done in foreign policy was the naval disarmament policy. England was having financial troubles maintaining her navy, and actually thought that since they were not going to fight the United States, they did not want to spend a lot of money producing a navy larger than that of the United States. Japan would have liked to have a navy larger than the United States but also could not afford it. The result was the international naval disarmament conference followed by a Treaty under which the 5:5:3 ratio for the navies of the three major naval powers was established. All three of these powers together with France and Italy agreed to stop building major ships until 1932. There was no restriction on light cruisers, and the Japanese immediately began a rapid expansion of their light cruiser forces. As a matter-of-fact these light cruisers played only a minor role in World War II, so the Americans lost nothing by this Japanese activity.

A second sizable diplomatic activity was the negotiation of the Kellog–Briand Pact which "outlawed" war. In my opinion, Kellog, the American Secretary of State actually thought that this pact would end wars among civilized powers. I should imagine that Briand, a fairly cynical Frenchmen, simply thought it was a way of improving relations with the United States as preparation for the next war. In any event, the pact was given a good deal of favorable attention in the American press and to some extent in the international press. The best that can be said about it is that it did no harm.

Nevertheless, the 1920s, were a fairly peaceful period. The usual collection of revolutions and local wars was going on in South America and indeed the war between Paraguay and Bolivia was quite a bloody affair. As I mentioned above, the marines were involved in various minor disputes in Latin America. I can remember a front–page color cartoon in the Chicago Tribune about the death of three marines in Nicaragua. Still these were very minor affairs and as I mentioned above, the Quaker Hoover took steps to minimize them.

The 1930s were dominated by the great Depression which was largely an American financial collapse which spread. France, however, also was involved. Austria wanted to join Germany, and the Bank of

France instituted a financial war against the Austrian banking system. This happened to coincide with the American Depression and made the depression even greater than it otherwise would have been.

Japan, interestingly enough, succeeded in largely avoiding the Depression, indeed 1933 was the boom year for Japan. A number of countries including the United States went off the gold standard and devalued their currency. Japan simply devalued their currency much more than anyone else with a result of their export prices fell sharply while domestic prices remained more or less stable in terms of the new devalued currency, and hence they had an export funded boom.

Chapter 14

World War II (Part 1)

The French army was generally believed to be the strongest and indeed it fought well in spite of the criticism after it lost a major battle in northern France. Their casualties in that battle were severe enough so that the remaining French army was badly outnumbered by the Germans. It had been smaller than the Germans even before its defeat in northern France, and rather weak in armor as indeed were most of the armies including such neutrals as Switzerland and Sweden. The Dutch and Belgian armies were, for small countries, sizable, and indeed fought well in the early days of the German march west.

The Germans succeeded in breaking through the Ardennes and trapped a significant part of the French army which never fully recovered from that loss. The renewed German attack was successful, and France surrendered.

Russia, of course, had a large conscript army with a fairly good tank corps. Japan had a large conscript army much of which was involved in China. They were, however, able to free forces for their southern invasions without much difficulty. When the war first broke out, it was widely believed that the French would have little difficulty holding off the Germans until they received adequate aid from England. A good many people have criticized the fighting capacity of the French army, but, in fact, it fought well, but was outmaneuvered.

In air power, an Italian general named Douhet had written a book in which he said that dominant air forces could win a war by destroying the industrial strength, particularly the armaments industry, of the weaker power. This book was very well written and was believed by the American and English air forces. As it turned out to be wrong. In consequence, Britain and the United States both had large air forces essentially designed for attacks on enemy cities.

The English, in this area, made a further mistake. They designed heavy and heavily armed, but not very fast, bombers with the idea that they would fight their way through the fighter defenses of the Germans. It turned out that they could not do so and had very heavy casualties when they tried. In consequence, they turned to night bombing which was less accurate, but was much safer for the crews of the bombers. The postwar studies indicated that Douhet was wrong.

The German Luftwaffe was almost the only major air force which was not taken in by Douhet. American air force officers criticized the Luftwaffe saying it acted as a sort of superior form of artillery in ground fighting. Their description was correct, but they should have congratulated them instead of criticizing. The giant bomber forces took up so much of the industrial power of the United States and

England that they actually were more damaging to the military supply system of their owners than to their opponents.

When it was obvious that France was finished, Italy entered the war, and demonstrated its military incompetence. Only the Viceroy of Ethiopia, a young prince of the royal family, showed any military talent at all. He expanded Ethiopia in areas where his small military forces had a good opportunity to inflict maximum inconvenience to the English. Eventually, of course, he was forced to surrender to the much larger available British forces.

Otherwise the Italians simply did badly. In an invasion of Egypt from the west they got about 70 miles through the desert and then dug in. They fortified themselves with a number of the U-shaped forts with the open end of the *U* in the direction away from Egypt. The English attack simply went around the sides of the forts and attacked the open end. The Italian forces collapsed and the English took much of Libya before the German reinforcement, commanded by Rommel, stopped them and indeed reversed their advance.

At the time, I was a high school student in Rockford Illinois and much interested in military theory, particularly naval theory. I thought the Italian navy was about to win a series of brilliant victories. The English fleet in the Mediterranean was about the same size as the Italian fleet. It was, however, divided with about half at each end of the sea. The Italian fleet was in the middle and was faster than the British fleet. They could have concentrated on one of the two parts of British fleet and, I thought, that there would be a very significant Italian victory. It turned out, however, that the Italian navy did not like fighting and never actually turned out in full force. Only at the very end when the Italians were commanded by a new Admiral did they win a minor skirmish. Negotiations for their surrender were much advanced at the time, so the Admiral who won accomplished nothing.

If Hitler had turned his forces to the Mediterranean, instead of Russia, or perhaps merely putting off the Russian invasion until the Mediterranean had been cleaned up, the war might have had a different ending. His minor efforts to conquer England by air power alone also failed. Altogether, the western powers gained a great deal from his military mistakes.

Chapter 15

The United States After 1890

With the finish of the Indian wars, the United States entered the modern period in its diplomatic history. From now on they made no serious effort to increase their own area or wealth by wars. Indeed, since the wars were expensive and they gained nothing material from them, they made a net loss from each one in terms of dead bodies and government expenditures. They could have made improvements in their resources by conquest since there were many large areas which were undeveloped or indeed almost uninhabited. As one example, the Amazon basin, which is similar in size to the Mississippi basin, but remains undeveloped, indeed, almost uninhabited. There are other similar areas. The island of Sumatra, for example. The Americans have never shown even the slightest interest in expansion into these empty areas.

What then did they do? The answer is they engaged in wars which were efforts to impose their ethical principles on the rest of the world. Whether this was a good thing or not is an open question. Personally I doubt it, but I am in the small minority in that opinion. In general the American people are very proud of their performance in these wars. If they judge merely in terms of military accomplishments, they have every reason to be proud. It is also quite possible that they left the world in a better state that it would have been had they not entered these wars. In order to judge this problem, they have to consider what would have happened had they not entered. Necessarily, there is a considerable amount of uncertainty in any such judgment.

As a whole, it is not obvious that the world is in a better state than it would have been had the Americans stayed out. It's easy, however, to offer reasons why their entry benefited themselves and the world in general. Certainly they changed the outcome from what would have occurred had they not been involved. Whether that is better or worse than the outcome if they had not entered is a question of which I have no answer. Certainly the standard history book implies that the Americans benefited the world and themselves by their participation.

Between the Wars

In the period between the two major wars, the U.S. military forces were involved in small-scale operations in places like Central America. At the moment the Latin Americans are highly critical of their participation. So far as I know there is no one who today praises it highly. The U.S. diplomats in general are vaguely apologetic about this area of their history. On the other hand, to say that they did bad rather than good is obviously just as speculative as saying that they benefited the areas in which they intervened. In any event, I propose to leave these minor operations aside. The marines and other American military personnel who suffered considerable casualties in these operations and, of course, the natives who also suffered casualties may object to this blank in my history, but it does not seem sensible to fill many pages with details on such trivial operations. Bemis gives them thorough coverage for anyone who is curious.

The small military forces in China did very little during this period. The gunboats were withdrawn just before the outbreak of the war with Japan, but since the withdrawal merely moved them to the Philippines, they were not really benefited. The infantry regiment in Tientsin was successfully evacuated before the outbreak of the war with Japan and the marine unit in Peking was on its way out when the war broke out. It was captured by the Japanese on the railroad between Peking and Tiensin.

Although the U.S. military did little in this period, the Department of State was not completely inactive. They maintained, and in fact expanded, their web of embassies and consulates. The most important single expansion was their recognition of Communist Russia. Since they had been refusing to recognize on political grounds, this was probably sensible, although it's hard to argue that their embassy was able to affect Communist policy in any way.

To give my personal opinion, these installations were much over-staffed. Getting rid of a large part of their personnel and in fact closing some of them down would in my opinion be a good move. When I was in the Foreign Service, I was not in favor of firing myself, but in retrospect I don't think I added much to the GNP. During much of this period, I was a specialist on North Korea and wrote various studies about what was going on there. The assignment of such a junior official as myself to be the principal expert on North Korea showed how little importance the government gave to that. Retrospectively, I think I did a competent job, but it is not obvious that the job should have been done. In fact, the bureaucracy in Washington, with which I later had much contact, got most of its information out of reading the newspapers, particularly the New York Times. I suspect that my much longer reports were not read by anyone of significance.

I was not involved with Latin America, but the U.S. policy there supported many foreign service officers, but did little else of value. This was during the period in which most South American countries had periodic revolutions. It was the U.S. custom to refuse to recognize the new government until it had been in power for some time. South Americans didn't like this and finally they agreed to automatically recognize immediately after a government was replaced. All of this kept a number of diplomats busy, but it's hard to argue it had any other significant effect.

Probably the Americans most significant diplomatic activity was the negotiation of reciprocal trade agreements with many foreign countries. Cordell Hull was a southerner, and like most southerners at that time thought that their protective tariffs were primarily aimed at protecting northern industry. At that time there wasn't much industry in the south. Getting their tariffs down was then, something that any southern politician would favor, and trading a reduction in other countries tariff rates for reduction in theirs seemed like a good bargain.

Substantially, all economists favored cutting tariffs. Henry Simons, my teacher, said that the United States should cut their tariffs, and if they could get other countries to cut their tariffs in reciprocation this would be a good thing. He, however, thought that the U.S. should cut theirs even if nobody else reciprocated. This was, of course, the conventional wisdom of economists. The principal victims of high tariffs are the citizens of the country that imposes them. But this is not, of course, the view of citizens who have not had a thorough grounding in economics.

The Department of State proceeded to negotiate a number of trades in which the United States cut their tariffs in return for cuts in other countries tariffs. This was beneficial, but I don't think that the Department of State fully understood the matter. They issued press releases pointing out that the U.S. exports to countries with which they had these tariff cuts increased more than their exports to the Americans. Looking at it as a common citizen who thinks the purpose of foreign trade is to export, this was a good thing. Most economists would regard it as irrelevant. Further, it clearly indicated that at least the public relations people in the Department of State understood the American public opinion, but not economics. Still, in net, they gained from the program, as did their partners in these agreements.

It is not generally thought of as a matter of foreign affairs, but the great Depression was an American catastrophe which was exported to other countries. There is no evidence that the American government or the Department of State were consciously engaged in either creating the Depression or exporting it. It was a catastrophe for the Americans as well as the other countries which caught the contagion from them.

Germany fell under control of Hitler and whatever else you can say about his policies he cured the Depression there. Since rearmament was a major part of his "cure", and this led to World War II, at a secondary level, the U.S. export of the great Depression was a very negative matter from the standpoint of foreign policy. Probably the great Depression and its spread to other countries was the most important international development of the 1930s. On the other hand, Japan by devaluing their currency created a local boom.

This was fine for them, but might have encouraged them into invading China. The United States took umbrage at the invasion. At first this merely meant that President Roosevelt made speeches in which he criticized Japan, Germany and Italy as aggressors. They clearly were, but it's not obvious that this was any of the American business.

Germany succeeded in annexing Austria and Czechoslovakia by diplomatic means although threats of violence were always in the background. Most accounts of this give partial blame to the British government for the elimination of Czechoslovakia. It should be kept in mind that England still had only a very small army. It would be rebuilt after England declared war on Germany.

Chapter 16

World War II (Part 2)

Hitler invaded Poland, and England and France declared war. Russia joined in the invasion of Poland and in fact acquired somewhat more real estate from the operation than Germany did. England and France did not declare war on Russia. Russia then began taking over the Baltic states which had been created at the end of World War I. The southern most three of them had little military power and quietly surrendered. Finland, however, had fortified their border which was also protected by a lake and decided to fight. To almost everybody's surprise, they were able to hold out for most of the winter. Eventually, of course, they had to give in and, rather surprisingly, Russia did not annex them, but contended itself with pushing the border back. Once again, England and France did not regard this Russia advance as a *casus belli*.

There was serious consideration in both England and France of sending aid to Finland. The Swedes sometimes claim that they won the war for the allies by refusing permission to the British and French troops to cross Sweden. I don't imagine any of my readers will regard this as well justified.

The Germans now attacked France, Belgium, and the Dutch. The French general staff had thought that the Ardaines forest was not passable by mechanized forces. The Germans thought it was passable and aimed their main blow through the forest. This permitted them to split the French army cutting off a large part of it and the British expeditionary force in the North. The British were able to evacuate their expeditionary force to England, although they had to leave most of their heavy equipment behind. When the French requested, the British used some of their shipping to move a good many French troops to the part of France that was not cut off by the Germans. Once again they had to leave their heavy equipment behind. The Belgian and Dutch armies were left behind, and in time, surrendered to the Germans.

At this point, the Allied forces in France were not only heavily outnumbered by the Germans, but were under equipped. Their surrender was more or less a necessity. Under the circumstances it was obvious that Italy would enter, which it did. Granted the ineptness of the Italian military machine, it is possible that Germany would have been better off had the Italians stayed out.

It is common to allege that German aggression caused the war. Note that in the early part of the war, Russia seized more real estate by military means than Germany. The English and the French failure to declare war on Russia has probably been wise, but raises doubts as to the claim that the German aggression caused the war in Europe. The Pacific war, of course, is another matter. Notably, the Russians did not enter until the Americans had defeated the Japanese.

Italy entered the war and demonstrated the incompetence of their army and navy. Beginning with the navy, I was in high school at the time and much interested in military matters, particularly naval. The Italian Navy was about the same size as the combined English fleets in the Mediterranean. The English had divided their fleet and had half the western end and half in the eastern. The Italian Navy was faster than the English and I, a high school student in the United States, anticipated a major Italian victory. It turned out, however, that the Italian Navy did not like to fight and hence never turned out in full strength. The English Naval Air Force succeeded in sinking a number of Italian Navy ships by an air raid on Taranto. The Japanese sent a special mission to study this attack, presumably as preparation for their upcoming air raid on the U.S. fleet.

In all other ways the Italians did badly except for the young viceroy of Ethiopia. He was a Prince of the Italian royal house and succeeded in using the small Italian forces in Ethiopia for several small offensives which caused considerable inconvenience for the British. Eventually, of course, he was forced to surrender by the superior British forces. It could be said, however, that he was the outstanding Italian commander of the war. That is weak praise, of course.

The Italians attempted to march east from Libya, but quickly displayed their military incompetence. The forces moved about 70 miles into Egypt and then proceeded to construct a series of small forts which were in the shape of a *U*, with the open end pointing westward. The British simply went around the closed-ends of the *U* and attacked from the rear. The Italian forces were almost wiped out. Hitler sent a moderate force commanded by Rommel which restored Libya, but was unable to seize the Suez Canal. It seems likely that had Hitler sent more troops, he would have come into control of the whole Mediterranean which would have made his position much stronger. This was one of a number of mistakes by Hitler, which contributed to his defeat.

The Germans had also attacked and defeated Yugoslavia and Greece. Their invasion of Greece followed an unsuccessful Italian effort. Altogether, the entrance of Italy into the war seemed to have handicapped Germany. If, however, Hitler had put larger forces into the Mediterranean, thus decisively beating the English forces and getting control of the sea, the war might have gone differently.

In passing I might mention that Franco, inadvertently, contributed to the Allied victory. Hitler wanted to attack Gibraltar thus giving the Axis control of the western Mediterranean basin and probably making it possible for them to easily take the eastern basin. Franco refused to permit the German troops to cross Spain even though he would, of course, have received Gibraltar, a long-standing objective of Spanish foreign policy. Franco, however, insisted that he would not give permission for German troops to cross and attack Gibraltar unless he was also promised a significant part of French–North Africa. There is no obvious reason why Hitler would not have permitted this, but he appeared to have thought he could cultivate good relations with France and hence refused to make the transfer. This was another of his mistakes which contributed to the Allied victory.

The United States, although not actually at war, was firmly on the side of the allies in Europe. It provided financial support and their destroyers began providing convoys for ships in the western Atlantic. It's even possible that they went far enough east so that the German submarines were seriously inconvenienced. There was even one case in which a destroyer and a submarine were engaged. Postwar investigations indicated that this was an accident with both commanders thinking that they were under attack.

In the Pacific, the United States was firmly on the side of the Chinese in their resistance to the Japanese invasion. Once again, however, this was not actual use of military forces but financial aid. Japan had no domestic sources of petroleum and depended on the Dutch East Indies for their supplies. The United States decided that the Dutch should cut off the source of petroleum, thus seriously injuring the Japanese operations. The English and the Dutch objected, pointing out that this might lead the Japanese to seize the Indies and in general push south. Roosevelt however insisted, and eventually they did embargo the Japanese.

It is necessary here to discuss the naval situation in the Pacific. The 1923 disarmament conference had left the United States with a navy which was markedly stronger than the Japanese Navy. Remembering the defeat of the Russians in 1904 because they had divided their fleet, the bulk of the U.S. forces were kept in the Pacific, specifically at Pearl Harbor. For rather mysterious reasons, President Roosevelt insisted on the transfer of one battleship division and half of the carriers to the Atlantic. They were of no use against the German submarines in the Atlantic, and except for one carrier which was eventually moved back to the Pacific, they spent the bulk of the war peacefully in harbor.

The Chief of Naval Operations realizing the situation was dangerous wanted to move the fleet to San Diego. There, it would have been safe against the type of attack delivered on December 7. The President fired him and then fired his replacement who also favored San Diego. Eventually, Roosevelt was able to find a Chief of Naval Operations, who was more cooperative with his foolish strategic ideas.

Right after the war, the Republicans gained control of Congress and held an investigation of Pearl Harbor in which they attempted to blame Roosevelt for deliberately arranging the death of many American sailors. As a political gesture, this was completely unsuccessful. Clearly it was a mistake, not a plot.

It should perhaps be said that Pearl Harbor is rather shallow, so shallow in fact that most of the battleship sunk simply rested on the bottom and were repairable, although it took several years. At that time it was thought that air dropped torpedoes could not be used in shallow water and Pearl Harbor was shallow. The Japanese had invented an air dropped torpedo which could be used in shallow water. One battleship made a normal procedure of going to general quarters at dawn and hence was fully prepared to defend itself. It was, however, sunk like the others which had not prepared. Another, the only one the Americans admitted was sunk, was sunk by conventional bombs rather than torpedoes.

All of the other battleships in harbor were resting on the bottom. One of them, an elderly one, had turned turtle and was also resting on the bottom but upside down. In the official American statement about Pearl Harbor, this ship was listed as seriously damaged. After two years of hard work, the repair effort on this ship was given up. The other ships which were resting on the bottom, but right side up, were eventually repaired but it took a long time.

The remaining carriers in the Pacific Fleet had been sent off to deliver the air garrison to the newly established military forces on Wake. They were returning to Pearl Harbor and in keeping with their normal routine had sent their airplanes off so that the pilots would get an extra day of leave in Honolulu. They arrived in an unarmed condition while the attack on Pearl Harbor was underway. The carriers themselves were well west of Pearl, and temporarily without planes.

President Roosevelt issued an order for the Pacific Fleet to "search and destroy" the Japanese task force. I presume the admiral in charge of the carriers had sensed enough to realize this "order" was intended for public propaganda in the United States, and successfully avoided the Japanese. If they had found him, he would have been sunk. The Japanese admiral, Nagumo, was not an air officer and made no effort to find the American carriers. I should say that two later cases in which the Japanese air reconnaissance failed were also under his command. Altogether he was a major asset for the United States and England.

It is interesting that the Japanese foreign office had arranged to have a war warning delivered to the Department of State before the attack on Pearl Harbor, although only a very short time before.

General Marshall promptly sent messages to places he thought most likely to be attacked. Why this warning was not received in Pearl Harbor, although it was received in Alaska and the Philippines, has remained a mystery.

Continuing with the Pacific war, the Japanese took advantage of the absence of the American fleet to push south. In general they did not annex these areas but they "liberated" them. Since the Philippines already had an elected government and the President joined MacArthur first on Bataan and then in the United States, they simply recognized the elected legislature and the head of the principal opposition party who took over the job of a President. No effort was made to punish him after the United States victory. I presume he did a good job.

In most other parts of the colonial empires, the Japanese removed the European occupying forces. In the case of the French Indochina holdings, they left the French in partial control. In Indonesia and Burma, they took the existing native opposition to the colonial empire, and installed them as rulers. Since at the end of the war none of these "puppets" were punished, I deduce that these governments were reasonably popular. Efforts by the former colonial masters to regain control all failed. The Japanese made no effort to conquer India, and the Congress party which was principal opposition to the British colonial forces apparently favored an invasion. Gandhi announced that he would welcome an invading force.

The English put all the leading members of the Congress party in jail and put down their efforts to cause disturbances by their followers.

This was not done politely. They machined gunned riots from the air. The Japanese had been able to seize a few Indians who were in Singapore as part of the British forces. They created in India Independence army from them, which of course was much too weak to accomplish anything much. After the war, the officers of this army were tried by the English and condemned to death, but the sentence was commuted by Mountbatten.

The British had moved a sizable fleet to the Indian Ocean and when Nagumo moved his fleet into the Indian Ocean, bombing Port Darwin on the way, it put to sea intending to fight. At the last minute, it realized how strong the Japanese were and took a course intended to avoid combat. Nagumo's reconnaissance was as usual poor and he failed to find them. For the rest of the war, the British fleet stayed west of India in order to avoid contact with the Japanese.

The United States using its remaining carriers in the Pacific established a convoy system to Australia and New Zealand. Japanese efforts to interfere with this led to a battle between carriers, which was more or less a draw. The Japanese, however, made no further significant efforts to interfere with the convoys across the South Pacific. The Japanese then attacked Midway, reasoning that the Americans would have to fight for it. They turned out they were right about this, but the American fleet inflicted a severe defeat on the Japanese fleet at that battle. As usual, Nagumo's reconnaissance failed. From then on the Japanese navy fought an essentially defensive war. MacArthur, moving north from Australia, seized a number of islands and took over most of the Philippines. He was preparing an invasion of Japan when Japan surrendered.

So much for the Pacific theater. In the Atlantic, a joint American-British force seized North Africa and invaded Italy. Meanwhile, of course, Hitler attacked Russia and after successes in the first two years began a steady period of defeat. The United States and England invaded France, thus sealing the fate of Germany.

The United States, however, had failed to understand the nature of the war. They had two enemies in Europe, Germany and Russia. As a result they permitted Russia to take over Eastern Europe, including half of Germany, without apparently realizing this was to their disadvantage. The outcome was one in which for the next few decades, the United States and the strengthened Russia were in continual controversy, fortunately not in actual war.

In the Pacific, Japan had been beaten and her forces were withdrawn from China and Korea. A civil war continued in China, and for reasons that are quite unknown to me, the Americans put the Chinese Nationalist under an arms embargo. I have never seen any explanation for this and indeed most histories don't mention it. It guaranteed a Chinese Communist victory since they were well supplied by the Russians.

Thus at the end of the war, the Axis powers had been beaten, and Russia had made substantial gains. The United States had made no material gains out of the war, but the American people seemed very happy about it. It led to a period of almost 50 years in which the

United States and Russia were on the verge of, but never actually formally, at war.[31]

The collapse of Russia, which was entirely an internal affair ended this lengthy and dangerous situation. The United States are now undoubtedly the only major power remaining, but they have not made very much out of that. They have had wars with minor countries four times, but have not won easy victories. The rapid growth of both China and India may mean that they will face strong rivals in 20 or so years.

At the end of World War I, the League of Nations was founded with the intent of insuring peace. The League was to a large extent an American idea and President Wilson pushed it very hard in Paris. He was unable to maintain control of the American government, however, and the United States refused to enter the League. Whether this was greatly important in the failure of the League to maintain peace is not obvious. They did get into the United Nations after World War II, but the postwar period has not been particularly peaceful. World War III has not occurred, but there have been a number of minor wars and many American soldiers killed.

But to return to the interwar period, the United States attempted to ensure peace by creating the Kellogg-Briand pact, which attempted to end war by making it illegal. I believe that Kellogg, the American Secretary of State, actually thought it would end wars. Briand, the French cosponsor, I am sure had no such beliefs. He probably

---

[31] Russian aircraft and American aircraft exchanged shots in North Korea during the Korean War.

thought it was valuable in that it made it more likely that the United States would enter on France's side in the next major war.

Communist Russia had the honor of being the first country to violate the pact. Almost before the ink was dry on the signatures, Russia carried out a small but undeniably military invasion of northern Manchuria. Russia owned a railroad running across northern Manchuria, and had a large collection of special privileges in connection with it. They maintained their own police force and in fact had military forces there also. The local warlord decided to assert Chinese sovereignty on the area, and Russia sent in more troops to stop him. Needless to say, this was the first, but not the only act of war violating the Kellog-Briand pact. Indeed the period after it was signed involved a number of minor wars and another major war, World War II. Altogether, making peace by international agreement is not a very successful method. The United States was not involved in most of the minor wars such as the Japanese invasion of China.[32]

The United States had, however, their own set of minor wars. Attempting to establish peaceful and democratic governments in Central and South America, they kept the Marine Corps and, to a lesser extent, the army busy. Before the end of World War I, they had invaded Mexico, but the troops were withdrawn in order to send them to Europe. The island of Hispanola, was divided into two parts,

---

[32] There was a minor brush between US gunboats on the Yangtze and the Japanese Air Force, but the Japanese apologized and paid damages, so it did not involve any serious casualties.

Haiti and the Dominican Republic. The army occupied the Dominican Republic and the Marine Corps Haiti.

The occupation of the Dominican Republic was more or less successful and when the United States withdrew a more or less stable dictatorship was established. After a considerable number of years, however, the dictator was assassinated and once again the American troops entered to pacify the area. A full division and a considerable number of naval vessels were dispatched, and with only a handful of casualties, peace was established. A respectable man was elected president and the area has remained stable since then.

Haiti has been a less successful operation. For a while it was under the control of a more or less stable dictatorship, but this was replaced by the chaos today. Altogether the U.S. interventions were not very successful. On the other hand, those South American republics which did not receive American expeditionary forces also have not done well although in recent years the situation seems to have stabilized. Needless to say, Latin American intellectuals do not give the United States credit for the present generally peaceful nature of Latin America. The Americans are indeed regularly denounced for their interventions. It cannot be claimed that they actually gained anything much from these operations, but it's hard to argue that without them Latin America would have been better off. Looked at from the standpoint of the United States, they were relatively cheap both in money and blood.

But the U.S. interventions in Latin America are a minor part of their foreign policy. With the end of the war in Europe, they once again attempted to establish an international body which would keep peace. This time it was called the United Nations. Realizing that it might take action which would be inconvenient for them, all permanent members of the Security Council were given veto powers. They were called great powers, but England and France let their empires dissolve so that now there is a vast gap between their power and the United States'. China was, as a matter of courtesy, listed as a great power. It is growing rapidly, however, and they may genuinely be a great power in the not distant future.

In immediate postwar period, there were two genuine great powers, the United States and Russia. Russia, however, collapsed and the present situation where there is only one great power, the United States is apparently stable. China and India are, of course, rapidly growing and may establish themselves as great powers in another 20 years. Japan and Germany might also recover, although at the moment both of them seem to be dominated by pacifists. The United States is the only genuine great power at the moment, but in practice their military forces have not done very well.

They have fought four minor wars with four minor opponents. In spite of the weakness of their opponents they have not clearly won. I should say that I'm not arguing their troops do not fight well or that their equipment was poor. Nevertheless, the outcome in all these cases was much less than a complete victory. Indeed, one of them, the Iraqi mess, is still going on. Let's take them up one at a time, beginning with the first and the biggest of them, the Korean War.

During the latter part of this war, I was in the U.S. embassy in Korea and indeed their principal specialist on North Korea. Notably my specialty did not represent great knowledge but simply the fact that no one else was interested. I depended primarily on intercepts of North Korean propaganda broadcasts. This was a poor source, but I knew more about the place than anyone else did. Note, I received only their propaganda output. The Armed Forces maintained a large radio intercept service which was intended to decode their internal messages. I don't know how successful this was.

At the time I thought the North Koreans had started the war on their own. One of the results of the overthrow of the communist party of Russia was that their internal correspondence and records had been very largely published. It is now known that the war started after a careful discussion between Stalin, Mao, and Kim. They agreed that China would necessarily enter and that air cover would be given by the Russians. Stalin insisted, however, that his aircraft stayed far enough north so that if shot down they would fall in Communist con-trolled areas. This meant that the air fighting took place well north of the ground fighting. It also handicapped the U.S. fighter planes who had to preserve enough fuel to return to base after the combat. This meant they had to fight while somewhat heavy with the additional fuel. In spite of this handicap, they were very successful. Apparently, the Russian planes were not very good. In any event, the Americans maintained control of the air, but it was not as important as one might have hoped.

By agreement with the Russians, the 38th parallel was the line of demarcation between the Americans, part of Korea and theirs. If you consider Korea as only the peninsula, this was a fairly even division. Korea, however, also contained a sizable amount of real estate between Manchuria and the sea. This went to Russia with the result that they held more of the real estate shown on the maps as Korea than the United States did. They also cheated a little bit on the actual demarcation of the borderline.

Both the United States and Russia established governments in their zones which were at least nominally independent. In the inter-war period, Russia had deported a sizable Korean colony from eastern Siberia to the center of Russia. They did not appear to have treated them very well in central Russia, but they brought some of them back and put them into the puppet government established in North Korea to keep an eye on the rest of the Koreans in that government. Kim Il Sung who had allegedly conducted a guerrilla campaign against the Japanese forces in Korea and Manchuria was made puppet dictator. When the Chinese Communists had established themselves firmly in China they showed signs of wanting to reestablish the traditional Chinese control of Korea.

In South Korea the situation was more complicated. Syngman Rhee had been part of the Korean effort to break away from the Japanese empire right after World War I. He had in fact been sent to Shanghai to make contact with the outside world and in fact act as a sort of Foreign Ministry for the rebel group. When the Japanese put down the rebellion in Korea, he went to the United States where he picked up a Ph.D. in Divinity from Princeton. He got back to Korea almost immediately after the American troops had arrived. He was of course completely dependent on the Americans, but he was clever and a Korean patriot.

His relations with the Americans were never good and indeed most of the high-ranking Americans with whom I had contacted hated him. He was, however, popular among the Koreans and won a number of elections without cheating. This does not mean that his followers were popular and indeed the elected legislature tended to be dominated by people who didn't like him. Altogether it was a difficult problem and I don't think the United States handled it well. On the other hand, I had at that time, and for that matter now, no real suggestions for solving the problem. Fortunately none of the high American officials asked my advice on the matter so I am free from the responsibility.

A democratic government was established and Rhee easily won the presidency. The Legislature, however, was by no means under his control and indeed many individual members of it expressed a general dislike of him. Nevertheless, the government existed and on the whole did well. President Rhee worked to insure that a great deal of money was put into education, and in the long run this might have paid of in economic development. While I was there, there was little effect of this sort, but necessarily it's a long run investment. The current flourishing of the Korean economy may be an outcome of his educational efforts.

The Russians in occupation of the north established a puppet government (without free elections) and provided it with an army. The Americans provided the equipment for an army in the south. The northern army occasionally used artillery to fire across the border into South Korea. South Koreans naturally replied. The only thing that United States did about this was to urge the South Koreans not to reply. The motive for this advice is not clear, but it may have been simply a counsel of desperation. Short of starting a war, the United States could do nothing other than give bad advice. As a very junior diplomat in the Far Eastern Service, I thought the advice was silly, but had no good idea of what they should do.

Eventually the north started a full-scale invasion. The South Korean army had not been built up by the United States so that it was strong enough to hold off the Russian equipped northern army.

The Korean army, such as it was, and the few American troops in Korea fell back to a position in South Korea around Inchon. MacArthur, who had spent the Pacific war with a series of usually small naval landings against areas held by the Japanese, arranged another landing in North Korea. The North Korean army collapsed and fell back north. The American forces reached the Yalu and the South Korean army on their right moved much farther north indeed almost to the Russian frontier. The Chinese were now prepared to enter and had taken a sizable army across to the woods on the right of MacArthur's position.

The pathologically stupid chief of intelligence for MacArthur's forces did not notice it. Indeed I, at that time a student at Cornell, knew the Chinese were in two days before G2 figured it out. The U.S. forces had captured several Chinese soldiers and their newspapers reported that fact. This meant to me that the Chinese were in, but the U.S. pathologically stupid chief of intelligence in the Far East, told reporters that these were merely stragglers.

The Chinese fell on the right flank of the U.S. army and it fell back in considerable disorder. The commanding general of the American forces in Korea was riding in a jeep which was following close behind a truck. On the truck was a piano which the troops had "liberated" in the north. It fell off and killed the general. So far as I know this is the only case in history in which a general was killed in combat by having a piano fall on him.

The new general who replaced him was able to restore order to the troops and establish a new line south of Seoul. He not only held there, but was able to push north and take back Seoul.

North of Seoul, however, the peninsula widens and the American generals felt they did not have enough troops to establish a firm defensive line across this wider part of the peninsula. It should be kept in mind that during all this time they were preventing President Rhee from expanding his army. He conscripted a lot of troops, but had no military equipment for them and the United States refused to give him any. This was only one of the many cases in which the U.S. command was pathologically stupid.

The war then wound down, and an armistice was eventually agreed on. South Korea remained a democracy. North Korea became a particularly unpleasant dictatorship. In the north, bad government led to considerable suffering and indeed a perfectly genuine famine. The South, by Asiatic standards, was moderately prosperous. President Rhee continued winning elections and various opposition candidates succeeded in getting into the Legislature. Once the war was over, the United States permitted him to expand his army.

After a number of years, President Rhee was replaced by a military coup. The general who organized the coup turned out to be an efficient manager and South Korea began the industrial development which eventually led to it being a major industrial power. The military dictator, however, was assassinated one night at dinner by his police chief. The police chief had failed to organize his followers and was arrested shortly after the assassination. South Korea then returned to an elected government, which continued the rapid economic development of Korea.

As far as I can see, the American government did almost nothing about this. They approved in general the economic development of the country and its democracy, but did little to help it. The continuing hostility between the two halves of Korea never led to actual warfare. The South's economic development continued rapidly, and the North had a long series of economic difficulties including a genuine famine. The South has built up a sizable army with a large organized reserve. If the United States had permitted them to do the same while the Americans were fighting a war on their side, perhaps the Americans would have won.

The Korean War was the first and most deadly of the wars the Americans had fought since the end of World War II. For a while the

United States and Russia were the two dominant powers in the world. The European colonial empires were all dissolved. In some cases the natives organized rebellion and cost enough casualties so that the Europeans decided not to continue fighting. More commonly, however, the withdrawal of the Europeans was voluntary. To take that one example, de Gualle in his prewar book "Le Armée de Métier" had expressed a desire to get out of all of the empire except Tunisia. When he became dictator of France, a revolt in the colonies was underway, principally in Algeria. He gave up the empire everywhere except in Algeria, and then, after a period of fighting, gave up there also.

Most of the remaining empires were given up without much fighting although the French fought to hold Indochina, which eventually became the U.S. responsibility and there was a sizeable upsurge in Indonesia. In general, the political left in Europe disapproved of the Empires. When they came into control of various European countries, they withdrew troops. As a rough rule of thumb, former colonies are less prosperous and well ruled than they had been when they were under control of the European democracies. In most cases the new government were not democratic either, although there are some outstanding exceptions. India, for example, was democratic and with the replacement of the Congress Party by its opposition a few years ago, it began fairly rapid economic development. Altogether, the seizure of the colonies in the 19th-century and then their abandonment after World War II, is a bit of history for which it is hard to offer a rational explanation.

As I mentioned above, the Korean War was the longest and hardest fought, in terms of casualties, of the wars the United States they fought since we became the world's leading power. Let me now take up the other three. It should perhaps be said that one of these is the war in Vietnam, and in this case the United States simply replaced the French who were trying to subdue a native rebellion. In the other three wars, although the Americans had military help from their allies, basically they provided the bulk of the military power. Altogether, as in the Korean War, they didn't do very well. To return to a theme expressed earlier, it is surprising that a country which, since the collapse of Russia has been generally regarded as the world's leading power, tends to do badly in wars with minor opponents.

The first Iraqi war was quick and easy. The dictator of Iraq decided that he would annex a small Arab country to his South. The United States objected as did a number other countries which were importing oil from the small country. A coalition was formed and easily and quickly booted the Iraqi dictator out of the small country. At that time there was no effort to replace him as ruler of Iraq.

The second war, mentioned above, was fought in former French Indochina and the United States didn't do very well. In essence, the French had attempted to set up a democratic government to replace their own empire in the area. They were obviously failing and the Americans entered to do the same thing. The communists in the area, however, with aid from Communist China on their northern border, resisted and caused the Americans a great deal of trouble.

After a good deal bloodshed, a peace was arranged in which the communists held North Vietnam and a democratic government, friendly to the Americans held the South.

The war was very unpopular in the United States and eventually all of their troops were withdrawn. They promised military help in the form of military supplies to the southern government, and at first provided them. The North which was heavily armed by the communists, attacked and the United States cut off the ammunition supply of the southern government which promptly collapsed. This was one of the worst foreign policy failures of the American recent history. It was, however, not solely foreign policy.

The draft was still in existence and people engaged in studying in a university were given a temporary exemption. This led to great many young men taking graduate courses which they actually were not interested in. They were unhappy about this and salved their consciences by demonstrating very vigorously against the war. This, together with a general public opposition to the war, obviously influenced the Congress. In any event, a great many people in former French Indochina, who had relied on the United States, were killed.

It may not appear to be a matter of foreign policy, but I think the wages paid to the U.S. soldiers and in particular national guardsmen war on active duty, should be sharply increased. Perhaps they should be doubled. So far there had been no difficulties with the U.S. troops in Iraq. Nevertheless, I think it would be desirable to sharply increase their wages. Partially this is a matter of justice. The Americans are expecting them to risk their lives to benefit the U.S. foreign policy and I feel that they should be generously compensated for this. It's easy to find cases where the U.S. federal budget could be cut with no social cost or indeed even with benefit. This would provide the money for higher salaries for the troops.

The United States are now engaged in their fourth minor post-World War II war. In my opinion it has been very badly managed. In the first place it was based on poor intelligence. Apparently, the United States CIA and its fellow intelligence organizations among their European allies all thought that Iraq was making nuclear weapons. Granted the number of countries that have such weapons, this was an obvious *casus beli*, but in any event the United States discovered they were not doing so when the U.S. troops overran their country. It was a quick and not particularly bloody war.

The two sons of the dictator chose to defend the family property against the army and were killed. Saddam himself hid in a hole in the ground but was eventually betrayed and pulled out of his hole by the American troops. He was tried by an Iraqi court and hung. His army and police did not attempt to defend him. There is no evidence that he was involved in the terrorism, which was organized and led by a wealthy Arab named Bin Laden.

Unfortunately the United States is also in another war, against terrorism. This war started when two groups of suicide bombers crashed American passenger planes which they had seized into the twin towers in New York City. About 3000 Americans died in this attack, and of course the United States lost the two buildings. This was apparently organized by Bin Laden. It seems highly likely that if they had not engaged in any counter action, further terrorist attacks would have been launched. Apparently, it is not particularly difficult to incite occasional Arabs into engaging in suicide attacks on Americans or on Arabs who are friendly with Americans.

It is notable that as of the time of writing the total number of American soldiers killed in suicide attacks, mainly in Iraq, is about the same as were killed in New York. Notably a great many Arabs have been killed as a sort of byproduct of suicide attacks on American troops who are often near Arabs. The attacks on Americans in Iraq are continuing so that by the time you read this the death toll may well be much higher.

The American death rate, very sharply less than the death rate on the U.S. highways, continues to cause concern. By coincidence on the day which I wrote this section of my book, the Washington Post had a full two-page spread of pictures of American soldiers who were killed in action. Needless to say, they did not show pictures of the far more numerous Arabs who were killed as a sort of byproduct to the attacks on the Americans. They also did not show the much more numerous victims of traffic accidents.

The war is not popular. Indeed it is like the Vietnam war in this respect. The Congress has talked about cutting off funds, but has not so far done so. It ended the Vietnam War in a communist victory by cutting off funds, and I imagine the congressmen still regret that. In sum, I end this history on a depressed note. The U.S. troops are fighting well, but the foreign policy doesn't seem to give them a good objective. If the reader can suggest anything, and I imagine your congressman, would like to hear it.

Appendix on China

Among the minor wars there were several in China. After World War II, the United States fought a fairly major war against China and Korea. That'll be taken care of it's proper place but the Chinese history is worth presenting as background.

Chinese dynasties tended to die out in 200–300 years and be replaced after a period of confusion. Chinese historians tended to blame the failures on the influence of women and eunuchs. An almost classical example was the period from about 1850 to 1900. A young man succeeded to the throne, but he was seriously ill, apparently from syphilis. How somebody with access to any number of females, all of whom have been medically inspected, succeeded in getting syphilis is a mystery. One of my Chinese instructors told me in a shocked tone of voice: "He went outside the palace". In any event he lost power, and the empress dowager took control. Since she associated with eunuchs and her reign was very unsuccessful, the traditional view of the undesirability of control by women and eunuchs was confirmed.

At the same time that this occurred, there was another sharp deterioration of the situation of the dynasty. Because of rules mentioned above limiting the size of Chinese ships, almost all trades between China and distant places like Europe and United States was carried on foreign ships. The clippers that sailed from Salem to Canton are part of the more romantic history of the U.S. foreign trade. In those days their merchant marine was a large part of their economy.

This was during the early part of the fluorescence of the U.S. navy and there was a regular squadron in the western Pacific. Although the opening of Japan was a major accomplishment of the squadron, in general it did very little in the way of assisting the U.S. diplomacy. One of the U.S. ships joined in the bombardment of the Taku forts by the British, but this was a decision of its Captain on his own.

The English interest in China was much more significant. There were a number of English and other merchants in Canton and in neighboring Macao. Some American merchants operated there also on a fairly large-scale. The British were, of course, the dominant nationality. These merchants in general had offices and storehouses along the bund. The Chinese officials felt them valuable commercially but disliked dealing with them. They tended to push them off to Macao. The Chinese officials apparently thought that these were hard people to deal with, having strange customs, and hence tried to get them to operate their own courts for the minor problems that arose. This was the origin of the foreign concession and extra territority system, although later it became radically different.

The English were more interested in one particular part of the foreign trade in the south. They raised opium in India and shipped it to China. The revenue derived from this was a significant part of the income of the British Empire in India. Smoking opium was illegal in China, as it is today in the United States. A new and crusading Chinese governor decided to stop this trade. He confiscated and destroyed all the opium he could find. The English were upset by this and began a war with China. This is called the "First Opium War" and the title is not a misnomer.

This was a bad time for China to get into a war with England. The steam engine had been invented and the new British warships normally had steam engines as well as sail. Further, their guns were much better than the ones the Chinese were using. As a result, the English won easily. This led to the establishment of several treaty ports farther up the coast of China and the establishment of extra-territorality for Englishmen in China. This was quickly extended to other countries. The Chinese favored this to get competition for the English. In addition, other navies with steam driven ships began to appear in Chinese waters. The Chinese stopped enforcing their anti-opium laws, which made the fiscal situation of India much better.

About 10 years later, a minor squabble took place on the deck of an English flag vessel with a mainly Chinese crew. None of the people who participated in the squabble are particularly reliable and hence the history of it is unreliable and will not be repeated here. In any event, England decided to renew the war, and the minor fighting which ensued once again demonstrated the incompetence of the Chinese military. In one area in which the Chinese were very competent, however. They made a net propaganda gain by calling it the "Second Opium War". The English called it "the Arrow War" after the name of the small ship on the deck of which it started. The term "Second Opium War", however, stuck and is used in most histories. As a result, there were more foreign concessions including one in Tientsin.[33]

The Chinese were also compelled to permit the establishment of foreign legations in Peking. The Chinese disliked these missions in Peking. The missions were neither fortified nor significantly garrisoned, although they tended to be located close to each other. Many of the foreign residents of Peking had weapons.

At this point an informal organization "The Fists of Righteous Harmony" usually called the Boxers, started a revolt against the "foreign" Manchu dynasty, but the Chinese officials succeeded in diverting it into an attack on genuine foreigners. This was a nasty affair in which a number of missionaries in isolated missions were tortured to death. The Boxers had the support of the empress dowager and a number of other high officials in the north. In south and central China where the officials had a better idea of a military strength of the west, the Boxers were suppressed.

In the north, the Boxers began attacks on the foreign community in Tientsin and Peking. The foreign communities in both cases were

---

[33] My first assignment in the Foreign Service was in Tientsin. My office and my apartment were in a large building in the former British concession. My tour of duty was enlivened when the Chinese Communist bombarded and captured the city.

able to defend themselves.[34] It's interesting that the Chinese regular army did not participate in the Boxer attacks on the foreign settlement. Since the regular army had artillery it would have been easy for them to win if they had tried. The empress dowager was favorable to the Boxers, and earlier had arranged to have the legitimate emperor murdered so she was in complete control. Thus, the refusal of the regular army to participate in the fighting was very fortunate for the foreigners, but rather mysterious.

Eventually, a foreign expeditionary force under the command of a German general was able to relieve Tientsin and fight their way up the railroad to Peking which they captured. The fighting was not very bloody, and the troops did a good deal of looting once they occupied Peking.

During the fighting in Peking, an American reporter living in Shanghai wrote and sent to New York an exciting series of dispatches on the massacres of the foreigners in Peking. Although they dominated the New York press for five days, he eventually admitted he had simply made them up.

As an amusing sidelight, the Chinese Foreign Ministry and their embassy in Washington maintained that nothing was happening. The Secretary of State took advantage of this by giving the ambassador a code message and asking him to get a coded reply from the legation in Peking. The message was delivered to the besieged locations under

---

[34] As an interesting minor fact, Herbert Hoover, a mining engineer, was employed in North China and participated in the defense of Tientsin. Since he was a Quaker, this was difficult for him. He carried a gun, but didn't use it.

a flag of truce and its coded reply was also collected and sent to Washington. Those people in the Department of State who felt that the Chinese were inscrutable, must have had their opinions reinforced by this incident.

The end product of this was a strengthening of foreign concession. The legation quarter was in essence converted into a fort, with foreign troops, including a marine company. In addition, the United States began maintaining an infantry regiment in Tientsin. They also sometimes had troops in Shanghai and a gunboat flotilla on the Yangtze. Other countries had more troops and gunboats. The Chinese were forced to pay reparations, although the United States gained some goodwill by returning some of the money. Altogether, the end product was a chain of foreign garrisoned settlements, each of which was governed by the law of its home country.

All of this seems most unusual but it should be pointed out that the Chinese central government was weak and in 1911 the child emperor abdicated. The usual period of confusion between dynasties followed, with warlord armies moving around China in efforts to establish a new dynasty. Although this was perfectly traditional in Chinese history, it, needless to say, made foreigners happy to not be subject to Chinese jurisdiction.

All of this complex structure protecting foreigners was wiped out in World War II. When I was in Tientsin, my office was in a large building which had been built by foreigners in the concession. One could easily tell where the concession ended by walking around in the streets and looking at the size of the buildings on each side of the street. The same situation existed in the other treaty ports. It should be noted that Chinese moved into these areas in great numbers because they did not want to be subject to warlord control. Further, there was reasonable freedom of the press in the concessions. Some Chinese intellectuals, while they opposed the system when it existed, had since shown signs of reconsideration. They pointed out that freedom of the press and freedom of speech existed in the concessions and hence intellectuals were not as suppressed as they had been before the concessions or had been since their elimination.

The Civil War continued until 1950. The concessions however were liquidated. The American garrisons were withdrawn from Tientsin before the Japanese occupied the place and the marine garrison from Peking was on its way out when the war broke out. They were captured by the Japanese. After the war and the defeat of the Japanese, the Civil War broke out again, of which more below.

But let me digress briefly again to the situation in China from 1911 until 1950. Although there was theoretically a government of China with its capital in Peking in the 1920s, actually the country fell apart with local governments and armies holding parts of it and fighting with each other fairly constantly. Peking, the nominal capital, in fact was conquered by these warlords three times in the 1920s. This led one historian to refer to the theoretical President of China as having a mediocre, but far from humdrum presidency.

Among the local governments, all of which claimed to be the national government. Sun Yat-sen and Chiang Kai-shek were largely in control of the area around Canton. They marched north, combined with the Communists, pushing minor warlords aside as they went until they reached the Yangtze River. They pushed down the river and actually reached Shanghai. At this point, the Communists decided to get rid of Chiang, but they managed it badly. The Communist Party was genuinely decapitated in the mud flats around Shanghai. There was, however, a remnant of the Communist Party holding an area south of the Yangtze River and Mao Tse Dung had the good fortune to be there and was able to establish his leadership for this fragment.

The Civil War went on and much of the American press coverage dealt with the fighting between the Chinese Communists and the Nationalists. This greatly exaggerated the Communist's importance. There were numerous other warlords, and the Nationalists were as much interested in suppressing various other warlords as the Communists. There was in fact another small area held by a second group of Communists.

Eventually, however, the situation of the Communists became very uncomfortable and they decided to go to a part of China closer to Russia. This led to the famous "Long March". The troops in the other communist area were to join with Mao's troops, but when they reached the rendezvous point, they found that instead of Communist troops, there was a Nationalist army waiting in ambush. This eliminated Mao's only serious communist rival in China.[35]

---

[35] The leader of the other group succeeded in escaping to Hong Kong where he was living when I was there. Unfortunately I never met him.

Recently a minor scandal concerning the Long March has been given considerable publicity. It is now claimed Mao Tse Dung did not actually walk along the route. He was, according to the present view, carried in a palanquin. I have no idea as to the truth or falsity of this allegation.

In any event, the Communist reached Yenan, a not very highly developed city located in a rather desolate area, but close enough to Russia so that supplies could be shipped to them easily across Mongolia which was at that time under Russian control. In fact the Russians did not send very much in the way of aid, but the area was distant and the Nationalist government then established in Nanking more or less left them alone. I should say that the Nationalist government was at the time attempting to suppress the other "warlords". A number of the leaders of various independent armies accepted commissions as governors of the area they controlled. If the Japanese had not entered at this point, a genuine national government might well have eventually been established.

The Japanese, however, could not be ignored. The young warlord of Manchuria who had succeeded his father after he had been killed by the Japanese attempted to take full control in southern Manchuria which was a Japanese sphere of influence. The Japanese responded by taking over that area while temporarily leaving the northern part of Manchuria under control of the Russians. I should say that the League of Nations appointed a committee to look into this matter and it came to the conclusion that the warlord's government had engaged in fairly vigorous anti-Japanese activities. Whether this was a full justification for Japanese operation is not at all obvious.

The north remained more or less under the Russian control and the warlord of Manchuria moved north. He was, of course, under pretty complete Russian control. This was however the 1930s and the great purges were in process. The Japanese decided that it would be safe to move into and take over the former Russian sphere of influence. Thus the whole of Manchuria came under their control and they set up a puppet government with the heir to the Manchu dynasty as a local emperor. The government in Nanking was unhappy about this, but for the time being, there was little they could do. The Japanese troops were also active in north China around Peking and eventually at a famous bridge mentioned by Marco Polo, there was an incident and the Japanese began a general invasion of the whole of China.

It is clear that the Japanese army in Manchuria, which was more or less free of control from Tokyo, was uncertain whether they should fight China or Russia. There were number of fairly serious battles between the Japanese army in Manchuria and the Russian troops in Siberia. Perhaps the largest single battle was at Nomohan, and the Russians clearly won. This may have decided that the Japanese should let the Russians alone and take over China. In any event, they began a serious invasion of that part of China, south of the Great Wall. Retrospectively, this was clearly a mistake. Japan could not mobilize enough troops to actually fully occupy China, and their efforts to establish puppet governments in general failed.

Another brief dip into the Chinese history may be helpful here. Several centuries earlier, a Chinese dynasty, the Ming, which was in a state of decay, was conquered by a barbarian tribe coming in from Manchuria. The Manchus then established the Ching dynasty which ruled China until 1911. This immediately raises the question of why the barbarian Manchus were able to establish a successful dynasty whereas the highly civilized Japanese were not.

This is particularly difficult to explain because China at that time was in a chaotic between-dynasty states which was called the period of the warlords. I think the explanation for this is that the Manchus were barbarians and realized that they were barbarians. They simply accepted the Chinese culture, indeed they had a number of Chinese troops in their armies and the Chinese scholars were invited to take official positions in their government.

So far as I know, historians have ignored this question. There were, it is true, Chinese scholars who refused to cooperate with the Manchus, but in general the scholar officials, mainly Chinese, set up a government very similar to that of a standard Chinese dynasty. There was no cultural conflict with the rather primitive Manchu ruling family.

Japan, however, had its own highly advanced civilization. They had taken many things over from China, including the characters and architectural style, but basically their government was radically different from the Chinese. Further, they had adopted European culture to a much greater extent than had the Chinese. Indeed, it was their technical superiority which made it easy for their army to defeat the remaining war-lords, particularly those allied with the so-called national government.

Things did not go entirely favorably for the Japanese. The Chinese national troops held them for quite a while on the highlands between the Yellow and Yangtze rivers.[36] The Chinese for a while prevented the Japanese navy from sailing up the Yangtze. Eventually, however, the Japanese broke through, and sailed up to Wuhan. Beyond Wuhan, however, the River runs through a set of gorges where the current is strong enough so that the Japanese navy would have found forcing their way up very difficult, and perhaps impossible. These gorges ran through a significant mountain range and the Japanese army decided not to push further. Chang Kai-shek established his capital in Chungking. Note that much of China remained under control of the various local rulers who had had control of individual provinces before the Japanese invasion.

The Japanese had control of Manchuria and part of China just south of the Great Wall. In addition, they controlled most of the coastal areas and a strip on both sides of the Yangtze. China had only a fairly light railway network and in general the Japanese controlled the railroads and narrow strips of land on both sides of them. There was one important railroad connecting the Canton area with Wuhan, and another to Kumning which the Japanese only took control of briefly in the very last days of the war. The area between the railroads,

---

[36] The commander of the Chinese forces here later became Ambassador to Korea. I met him when I was in the U.S. embassy there. In private discussions, he gave the full credit for the successful defense in this area to the troops, but obviously his lead-ership was also effective.

away from a coast, and away from the Yangtze remained under the Chinese control.

Although these areas were unimportant from the strategic standpoint, the area held by various local Chinese governments was large and had a large population. Normally, most of these areas were subject to officials who had been ruling them before the Japanese invasion and accepted by the national government in Chungking. Many of them, of course, were simply warlords who had held on to the areas before the Japanese arrived. The Communist remained in control of the area around Yenan, and made efforts to takeover various other areas from the Nationalist governors. This sometimes involved fairly serious fighting between the two Chinese governments.

With the surrender of Japan to the United States, these areas were taken over by various Chinese officials. Manchuria was certainly the best developed part of China at that time there was a rush by both the Communists and the Nationalists to get there. The Communist got there first, mainly because the Russians in control of Port Arthur refused to permit the American navy to land national troops. After a short delay, however, the Nationalist got in using a secondary harbor.

The Russians were equipping the Communist forces, but nevertheless at Ssuping Kai, the Nationalist won a major victory and the Communist forces were forced to withdraw from Central Manchuria to an area directly bordering Siberia. At this point, and this is somewhat mysterious, an arms embargo was slammed on the Nationalist by the American government. I have never seen any explanation for this, and indeed many historians don't even mention it. The Communist, of course, were being very well supplied with Russian equipment which was no longer needed elsewhere because the Germans had been beaten.[37]

The combination of the U.S. arms embargo and the Russian equipment meant that the Communists had little difficulty in taking over all of China, except Taiwan. The rather poor status of the national army might have meant that the Communists would have won even if the United States had permitted the Nationalist access to their arms supply. The United States didn't, however, and hence their defeat was certain.

The Nationalists did receive some arms from the United States. The American troops in leaving various islands in the Pacific left a lot of equipment behind. This was left unguarded in a tropical wet climate and with anybody wished able to take pieces of it. After a while, the Americans gave all of it to the Nationalists. They sent a technical mission out to look at it and it decided it was junk. The Nationalists sold it all at auction in the United States with bids being solicited for all of the abandoned American army equipment on a given island. They made about 200 million dollars, but this money was in the United States and hence could not be used to purchase ammunition for use in China because of the embargo. The money was, however, of considerable use to the Nationalists in other ways. The Americans offered no other serious assistance to the Nationalists.

With the outbreak of the Korean War, President Truman decided to order the navy to prevent a communist invasion of Taiwan, and at

---

[37] I was in Tientsin when the Communist took it over and remembered seeing the plentiful equipment held by their forces.

the same time to prevent a wildly unlikely invasion of the mainland by the national government in Taiwan. The Americans did not formally recognize the Formosa government and, after an unsuccessful effort to establish diplomatic relations with the Communists withdrew the U.S. diplomatic establishment from the mainland.[38]

[38] At the time I was a Vice Council in Tientsin. The Americans had little trouble with the Communist government which officially did not recognize the United States government. Still, on the whole I was glad to get out in one piece.

References

Adams, H., *The Education of Henry Adams* (Houghton Mifflin Co., Boston, 1918).

Bemis, S. F., *A Diplomatic History of the United State* (Henry Holt & Company, New York, 1952).

Boot, M., *The Salvage Wars of Peace* (Perseus, 2003).

Borneman, W., *1812: The War That Forged a Nation* (Harper, New York, 2004).

London, J. E., *Victory in Tripoli: How America's War with the Barbary Pirates Established the U.S. Navy and Shaped a Nation* (John Wiley & Sons, Inc., Hoboken, New Jersey 2005).

Wolf, L., *Little Brown Brother: How the United States Purchased and Pacified the Philippines* (History Book Club, New York, 1960).

Index